CHRIST OUR BROTHER

CHRIST OUR BROTHER

BY THE SAME AUTHOR:

THE SPIRIT OF CATHOLICISM
CHRIST AND THE WESTERN MIND

CHRIST OUR BROTHER

BY

KARL ADAM

PROFESSOR IN THE UNIVERSITY OF TÜBINGEN

TRANSLATED BY

DOM JUSTIN McCANN, O.S.B.

NEW YORK

THE MACMILLAN COMPANY

1931

Nihil Obstat
ARTHUR J. SCANLON, S.T.D.
Censor Librorum

Imprimatur
PATRICK CARDINAL HAYES
Archbishop, New York

March 11, 1931.

232 H
A19cEm

SET UP BY BROWN BROTHERS LINOTYPERS
PRINTED IN THE UNITED STATES OF AMERICA
BY THE FERRIS PRINTING COMPANY

TRANSLATOR'S NOTE

THIS book is a translation of Dr. Adam's *Christus unser Bruder,* a volume of essays and addresses published last year (1930) in a revised and enlarged edition. The first edition (1926) contained only four chapters, namely, the first three chapters of this volume and a fourth which is now included in the author's *The Spirit of Catholicism.* The publishers of both these editions are Messrs. Joseph Habbel of Regensburg (Ratisbon). To them and to the author the translator here offers his best thanks for the privilege of making this English translation.

In his *The Spirit of Catholicism* the author surveyed in outline the whole field of Catholic doctrine and piety, his purpose being to expound the nature of Catholicism and to show the essential unity which underlies its rich variety. In the present book his purpose and effort are quite different. He now takes one central doctrine of the Christian faith in relative isolation, and endeavours to bring this doctrine home to us in its reality and practical implications. Throughout this book there is practically but one subject, our Lord and Saviour, and practically but one aspect of that subject, the sacred humanity. Convinced that dogma is the very structure of the Christian life, Dr. Adam would have us meditate upon the doctrinal fact that our Lord is not only true God, but also true and perfect man. To that end he portrays "the man Christ Jesus" in His life and work, in His preaching and in His prayer. He is concerned also to show the vital connection of our Lord's humanity with His office of Mediator, and in a striking chapter enlists the majestic witness of the Roman liturgy in the service of his thesis. And he hopes that by better knowledge and more trustful love of "the first-born amongst many brethren" we may all be drawn into closer and more confident relations with Him and with our brethren through Him. In briefest summary the author's conviction is this, that a deep appreciation, not only of the divinity and transcendence of our Lord, but also of His humanity and fellowship with us is of essential importance for our Christian lives. It is in that conviction that he has written these chapters and called his book *Christ Our Brother*.

SAINT BENET'S HALL
    OXFORD
January, 1931

CONTENTS

CHRIST OUR BROTHER

CHRIST OUR BROTHER

CHAPTER I

JESUS AND LIFE

THE glory of His Father, the fulfilment of His divine will, the establishment of the Kingdom of Heaven: such were the aims of our Lord's human life. By the side of this divine purpose and pursuit of the 'one thing necessary,' there was no room for any ideal of a purely earthly character. 'He that hateth not his father, and mother, and wife, and children, and brethren, and sisters, yea and his own life also, he cannot be my disciple.' [1]

Indeed, it would almost seem that Jesus was so aflame with zeal for the glory of His heavenly Father that he disregarded and despised all earthly values and rejected that earthly life which is compacted of them; or, at least, that He regarded this earthly life and its interests as something in itself quite indifferent, and as related to the Kingdom of

[1] *Lk.* xiv, 26; *Mt.* x, 37.

1

Heaven only in a loose sense, as being the training
ground and battlefield of God's soldiers. So we
may fairly ask what was in fact the outlook of our
Lord's human mind, and what was its natural
tendency. Was He one of those mystics who, in
the fierce effort of their Godward ascent, strive to
put away from them all earthly desire and look
upon this world as a prison or as a place of exile?
What was His attitude towards the life of the
peaceful hill-country of Galilee, or of the turbulent
streets of Jerusalem, as that life flowed round Him
in gladness and in sorrow, in pleasure, pride and
power? Did He flee from that life—or did He
accept and master it?

There is no feature in their delineation of Jesus
which the evangelists bring out so plainly and
powerfully as His passionate devotion to His
heavenly Father, His unconditional surrender of
His whole being to the divine will: 'My meat is
to do the will of Him that sent me.'[1] But for
Jesus this Father was not the pale and distant deity
of contemporary Hellenistic philosophy, or of that
late Jewish theology which was so much influenced
by it. He was no remote God, sitting enthroned
above the clouds in solitary silence and maintaining

[1] *Jn.* iv, 34.

2

contact with men only through His angelic hosts;
He was the living God of revelation. Here our
Lord's teaching is linked up with the pure preaching of the prophets, wherein God was set forth
emphatically as the most living and most personal
presence and power. Jesus regarded His Father
as one who is ever active [1] and constantly working.[2]
It is He that sends sun and rain.[3] He clothes the
lilies of the field [4] and feeds the ravens.[5] No single
sparrow falls to the ground without the Father,[6]
and all the hairs of our heads are numbered in His
reckoning.[7] The qualities and talents of a man,
his 'pound,' are from God, and God will demand
back that which is His own.[8] Our daily bread is
the gift of our Father. Man belongs to God as the
sheep belongs to its shepherd and master,[9] and
depends on him for his very being and his every
act. And so, too, the destiny of man and of the
world is determined by the will of God. All
depends upon Him, the whole course of this world's
history with its wars and tribulations, to the very
end.[10] From Him come the leaders of mankind;

[1] *Cf. Jn.* v, 19.
[2] *Jn.* ix, 4.
[3] *Mt.* v, 45.
[4] *Mt.* vi, 30.
[5] *Lk.* xii, 24.
[6] *Mt.* x, 29.
[7] *Mt.* x, 30.
[8] *Mt.* xxv, 27.
[9] *Lk.* xv, 6.
[10] *Mk.* xiii, 32.

the prophets [1] and John the Baptist were sent by
Him. [2] Above all, from Him comes the Son.

That was what God meant to Jesus, and with
such a faith how could He give any but a second-
ary place to creaturely causality? Neither the rigid
course of natural law, nor any human energy,
could be regarded by Him as ultimate realities.
In all existence, in all activity, in every happening,
He pierced to the ultimate fact and saw the finger
of God. For Him there was absolutely nothing on
earth which was not completely controlled by the
divine will. For Him every single fact was an
embodiment and incarnation of the will of
God.

That being so, His attitude towards life and
towards its living values could only be a positive
and affirmative attitude, and indeed a profoundly
religious attitude. For to Him reality was not the
operation of some cold external necessity, or
soulless and inexorable destiny, but a manifestation
of mind and absolute freedom and perfect goodness, the work of His Father's will. For Jesus there
was no such thing as 'dead' nature. In mountain
and stream, in flower and in bird—and above all
in God's favourite, man—Jesus, with His soul

[1] *Mt.* xxiii, 24, 37.   [2] *Mt.* x, 10; *Jn.* i, 6.

4

immersed in God, recognized and hailed that same reality, the most living, the most profound, the most precious thing of all that He knew. And so His contact with the actual world was a contact with the will of His Father, and an immediate experience of the Wisdom, Goodness and Beauty of God. It was devotion, prayer, religion.

Hence came that love of nature which in its expression is so realistic, so devoted and so profound, as to ring completely modern. His parables, with their masterly delineation of the simple and the unnoticed, belong in their effortless sublimity to the greatest things of human literature. At one time He is rejoicing in the birds of the air, that 'sow not neither do they reap, nor gather into barns.' At another He is watching children playing in an Eastern street, and they pipe, and dance, and sing, and some of them sulk. Now He is thinking of the gladness of the young mother, who forgets all her pain in the joy of her new-born son. Again He sees the poor woman who has lost her groat: she lights a candle, and sweeps her house and seeks diligently until she finds it. Nothing is too small for Him. He takes the tiniest flower of the roadside, and lifts it lovingly up and up, like some divine forget-me-not, and makes it speak with a thousand tongues of God and of His loving care. Nor was His love for nature and natural things any merely sentimental enthusiasm such as was characteristic of the poets of the Romantic Movement. Of the love of nature for nature's sake Jesus knew nothing. For Him nature was nothing more and nothing less than a living manifestation of the will of God; and, in consequence, His love of nature was only one expression of His love for God and God's will. But just for that very reason was His love of nature so genuine and so wholehearted.

And if Jesus loved nature, He loved man more wholeheartedly still. Man's being was so pervaded by the will of His Father and so bound up with it, that it was impossible to love God without loving man also. The Old Testament set down separately the two commandments: Thou shalt love God, Thou shalt love thy neighbour. Jesus ran the two into one: 'All things therefore whatsoever ye would that men should do to you, do ye also to them. For this is the law and the prophets.' [1] Love of our fellow-man is but another aspect of our love of God. And just as our Lord could not love nature for nature's sake,

[1] *Mt.* vii, 12.

even so His love of man was no love of man apart
from God. He loved man because God loved
him. It was this high quality, as Nietzsche
recognized, which gave His love its wholesome
balance and its delicate refinement. And the same
quality of His love made it something utterly
genuine, personal and delicate, as genuine and as
deep as His love for His Father. 'And he took a
little child, and set him in the midst of them: and
taking him in his arms, he said unto them . . .'[1]
How well He understood the grace of sympathy.
He could make His own the anguish of a father's
heart,[2] the hopeless sorrow of a desolate mother,[3]
the distress of an invalid.[4] See how He dealt with
the woman taken in adultery, with repentant
Peter, with the Good Thief. Is there anywhere
else in the whole Gospel such sweet gentleness and
such charming delicacy, both in what He says and
in what He does not say? And how His soul was
touched when He encountered human pain! The
Gospels tell us over and over again that He had
compassion on the multitude.[5] It was characteristic of Him and it had deeply impressed His

[1] *Mk.* ix, 35.
[2] *Cf. Mk.* v, 36.
[3] *Lk.* vii, 13.
[4] *Mt.* ix, 2.
[5] *Mt.* ix, 36; xiv, 14; xv, 32;
Mk. i, 41; *Lk.* vii, 13.

disciples. Jesus many times rejected the petitions of strangers;[1] but never an appeal for help in need. 'And he healed them all.'[2] Not seldom He did not wait to be asked.[3] He preferred to break the Sabbath and scandalize the Pharisees rather than refuse help.[4] He could not endure to see misery; He could not eat His bread in the Pharisee's house until He had healed the sick man who was present there.[5] And see how He spoke to those in pain, addressing them in the simplest and tenderest words: 'Son,' says He to the man sick of the palsy;[6] 'Daughter' to the poor woman with the issue of blood.[7] And when He sounded the very depth of human wretchedness, as at the grave of Lazarus or before the doomed city of Jerusalem, then, the Gospel tells us, He 'groaned in spirit and was troubled,'[8] and 'seeing the city, he wept over it.'[9] Indeed, His life and His miracles are a history of love breaking victoriously through the greatest obstacles. And so completely

[1] *Lk.* xii, 14; *Mk.* v, 19.
[2] *Cf. Mt.* iv, 24; *Mk.* vi, 56; *Lk.* v, 17, *etc.*
[3] *Mk.* i, 25; iii, 3; v, 3; x, 5, *etc.*
[4] *Mk.* i, 23; iii, 2; *Lk.* xiii, 14; xiv, 3; *Jn.* v, 9; ix, 14.
[5] *Lk.* xiv, 2.   [6] *Mk.* ii, 5.
[7] *Mk.* v, 34.   [8] *Jn.* xi, 33.
[9] *Lk.* xix, 41.

8

did he identify Himself with love, that He could declare that we do to Him whatever we do to the least of His brethren.

How different Jesus is in this respect from the stern figure of St. John the Baptist, as the Gospel brings him before us, from whom we hear little of love, but much of penance. And it is possible for us to push asceticism so far that we lose all feeling and sympathy for others. But Jesus did not yield to this tendency. He left the wilderness and went among men. He had an eye not only for the wickedness and sin of the world, but also for its suffering. And with all its wealth and breadth of sympathy His heart went out to man and to his suffering.

And it went out also to his joy. And this indeed is a fact which throws the clearest and plainest light upon our Lord's manner of regarding life. The creed of the stoic Emperor, Marcus Aurelius, was 'Sustain and abstain.' To the neo-Platonists the body was the soul's prison, and death an escape. To the ancient Egyptian solitary duty seemed comprised in the terse command: 'Flee, be silent, weep.' And in the time of Jesus the would-be 'righteous' and 'separate' Pharisees had similar views of life. Following the 'tradi-

9

tions of the ancients'[1] they had added to the five
great national fasts by appointing weekly fasts on
Mondays and Thursdays, and by their severe rules
for fasting they had cramped all joy. And the
Gospel tells us that St. John the Baptist and his
disciples fasted strictly. But Jesus of set purpose
and deliberate intent rejected the requirements of
this code.[2] It was not fasting itself that he
rejected—for He had Himself fasted forty days in
the wilderness—but the dispositions in which
these facts were practised. The Jews kept fasts
in memory of grievous national calamities, and
indulged themselves in sadness and despondency.
Jesus censured such dismal fasting. 'But thou,
when thou fastest, anoint thy head.'[3] He esti-
mated the value and worth of fasting, as of all
other devotional exercises, according to the intention of the heart. He would have it done in gladness of heart with a pure and joyful acceptance of
God and of His fatherly will.

When fasting depresses and paralyses the soul,
then it no longer does it any good. And His
disciples, the 'friends of the bridegroom,' do not

[1] *Mt.* xv, 2, *sqq.; Mk.* vii, 3, *sqq.*
[2] *Cf. Mt.* xi, 18; *Lk.* vii, 33, 34.
[3] *Mt.* vi, 17.

fast 'so long as the bridegroom is with them.' [1]
So our Lord's rejection of the mortifications of the
Pharisees was a deliberate rejection of that dismal,
cramped and violent asceticism and a decisive
adoption of a freer and gladder attitude. 'Have
you not read what David did when he was hungry,
and they that were with him: how he entered into
the house of God and did eat the loaves of propo-
sition?' And should the children of the household
be forbidden to take that which their Father offers
them? [2] So Jesus, too, took His share unaffec-
tedly and without embarrassment in the little joys
that day brought after day. He suffered Himself
to be invited and He went to dinner, even though
His enemies in their malice would call Him therefore a 'glutton and a wine-bibber.' [3] Banquets
were given in His honour, whether by Levi [4] or
another Pharisee.[5] At another time He was in the
intimate family circle of Simon and his wife's
mother,[6] or with the busy Martha; [7] or He invited
Himself to the table of Zacheus.[8] He worked His
first miracle for the guests of a marriage feast,[9]

[1] *Mt*. ix, 14.   [2] *Mt*. xii, 4.
[3] *Mt*. xi, 19.   [4] *Lk*. v, 29.
[5] *Mk*. xiv, 3; *Lk*. vii, 36; xi, 37; xiv, 1.
[6] *Lk*. xix, 6.   [7] *Lk*. x, 38; *Jn*. xii, 2.
[8] *Lk*. xix, 6.   [9] *Jn*. ii, 10.

11

and it is significant that He frequently found the framework and material for His parables in the happy banquet [1] and the sumptuous marriage feast.[2] He envisaged the glory of eternity itself as a sitting down to table with Abraham, Isaac and Jacob.[3] And His final and greatest gift to His disciples before His death was a love feast, the feast of everlasting communion in His Body and Blood.

Away then with Nietzsche's supposition, that Jesus never laughed. How is it possible that He should not Himself have known a deep and pure joy, who was preaching the glad gospel of the Father, and who in all joy and in all sorrow recognized God's infinite power and goodness? Jesus loved men and loved their life in the will of His Father. He was drawn to man not merely by His tears, but by His laughter also.

And again it was through His Father's will that Jesus came profoundly into touch with the darker side of our humanity, its folly and sin, its pettiness and misery. There was no eye so keen as His for the wretchedness of poor humanity:

[1] *Lk.* xv, 22; xii, 19; xiii, 26; *Mt.* viii, 11.
[2] *Mt.* xxii, 11; ix, 15; xxv, 1; *Lk.* xii, 36.
[3] *Mt.* viii, 11.

'If you then being evil . . .';[1] 'O generation of
vipers, how can you speak good things, whereas
you are evil? . . .';[2] 'an evil and adulterous
generation seeketh a sign.'[3] We seem to hear in
these words an undertone of a deep, secret
antipathy towards this depraved and distorted
humanity. And yet He knew that even this poor
humanity was not without some sort of inward
relation to the will of His Father. And therefore
could He 'suffer' it yet further. And His soul
was attuned to the sublime melody of unwearied
patience with the miseries of men. The cockle
must not be torn up, but must be let grow, even to
the day of God's harvesting. We must not call
down fire from heaven upon the unbelieving
cities. The Father sends His sunshine and His
rain upon just and unjust alike. And since everything depends on the Father, therefore 'Judge
not!' We cannot here and now, in this world,
separate the 'Just' and the 'Sinners.' The son of
Abraham, even if he be a priest or Levite, is not
always better than the Samaritan. Abiding again
by the will of His Father, Jesus rose majestically
superior to all the perversities of human civiliza-

[1] *Mt.* vii, 11.   [2] *Mt.* xii, 34.
          [3] *Mt.* xii, 39.

13

tion, to all moral, social and national distinctions and divisions. And He stood also outside all economic and political conflicts. He would have nothing to do with questions of inheritance.[1] We must give to Caesar the things that are Caesar's.[2] 'Peter, put up thy sword into its place.' [3]

What then was His attitude towards life? There was in Him no world-weariness, no strengthless melancholy, no timid shrinking from the fray. He looked reality full in the face, and gripped it with both His hands, and with His whole heart accepted it. There was no part of reality which He tried violently to explain away, or to shut His eyes to. Jesus was no dreamer. He was a realist, utterly alive to all the facts, to the full, complete reality, whether that reality were light or darkness. Nor was His devotion to natural things and to man any mere 'love to order,' any mere act of obedience to God which left His heart indifferent.

For the will of God and natural things were not for Jesus two separate and disjointed factors, only conjoined in a purely external manner. On the

[1] *Lk.* xii, 14.   [2] *Mt.* xxii, 21.
[3] *Mt.* xxvi, 52.

14

contrary the will of God was manifested in things and through them. Therefore, in loving the will of God, He was loving things also, in the very centre of their being. He felt Himself one with all reality, in a union that was formed and maintained by that living might of God's will which was manifest in all.

But, on the other hand, for the very reason that reality had no meaning for Him but as an expression of His Father's will, His love for reality was taken up into His love for His Father. His relation to reality was strictly dependent on His relation to His Father. And therefore He never surrendered Himself unreservedly to it. An earthly attraction which should conflict with the will of His Father—such a thing could not touch the soul of Jesus. His life-zest was ennobled and transfigured by a marvellous steadiness of soul, a sure loftiness of sentiment and thought. His long fast in the wilderness. His vigils, the poverty of His wandering life, the labours of His preaching, His ministry to the poor and outcast, the maturity and distinction of His manner towards His malicious opponents, above all the heroism of His life and of His death—these things can be understood only if we realize that He was ever and in all circumstances the captain of His soul. He possessed Himself fully; He was not subject to the things amid which He lived; but living among them remained ever completely Himself.

Jesus did not flee from life, nor yet was He subject to life: Jesus mastered life.

CHAPTER II

JESUS AND PRAYER

FROM the writings of our modern critical theologians I select the following testimonies regarding Jesus and prayer. 'Jesus is the inaugurator of a new epoch in the history of true interior prayer.' [1] 'Genuinely interior or personal prayer is really the creation of Jesus.' [2] 'History records no one who prayed with such power as Jesus.' [3] The prayer of Jesus in Gethsemane is 'the most profoundly religious utterance that has ever been spoken.' [4]

Having quoted these testimonies let us now endeavour to illustrate them by investigating the inner character of our Lord's prayer. It is curious, we may remark in passing, that Heiler, who speaks so emphatically regarding the importance of that prayer, should yet in his own valuable treatise on prayer devote only a few lines to it.

[1] *Heiler.*   [2] *Söderblom.*   [3] *Wernle.*
[4] *Hoffding.*

17

The gospels agree in portraying our Lord's earthly life as a life of prayer. That first public testimony which His Father bestowed upon Him, just as He was entering upon His public life, came to Him while He was in prayer. 'Jesus also being baptized and praying, heaven was opened.' [1] In the course of His ministry He retired constantly to refresh Himself in quiet intercourse with His heavenly Father. 'And rising very early, going out He went into a desert place: and there he prayed.' [2] 'And he retired into the desert and prayed.' [3] 'And having dismissed the multitude he went up into a mountain alone to pray. And when it was evening he was there alone.' [4] Over and over again do the evangelists tell us of this quiet, solitary prayer.[5] St. Luke especially notices it. St. Matthew and St. Mark tell us that when Jesus sought the Mount of Transfiguration, He took with Him three trusted disciples and led them 'up into a high mountain apart.' St. Luke adds that He went up in order to pray. 'And it came to pass about eight days after these words that he took Peter and James and John, and went up into

---

[1] *Lk*. iii, 21.
[2] *Mk*. i, 35.
[3] *Lk*. v, 16.
[4] *Mt*. xiv, 23.
[5] *Lk*. ix, 18; xi, 1; *Mt*. xxvi, 36.

a mountain to pray.'[1] From St. Luke also we learn that the choosing of the apostles was prepared and sanctified by vigils and prayer. 'And it came to pass in those days that he went up into a mountain to pray, and he passed the whole night in the prayer of God. And when day was come he called unto him his disciples.'[2] All the evangelists lay stress on the point that Jesus worked His Messianic miracles in the power of prayer. According to St. John, when He stood before the grave of Lazarus He prayed thus: 'Father, I give thee thanks that thou hast heard me. And I knew that thou hearest me always.'[3] Jesus Himself regards the miracle as an answer to prayer. St. Mark, too, testifies that when healing the deaf-mute Jesus 'looked up to heaven and groaned' before He said 'Be thou opened'; [4] and that when they brought Him the lunatic boy, He declared: 'This kind can go out by nothing but by prayer and fasting.'[5] And all four evangelists tell us that He introduced the miracle of the multiplication of the loaves with thanksgiving and blessing.[6]

And not only His Messianic miracles, but His

[1] *Lk*. ix, 28.
[2] *Lk*. vi, 12.
[3] *Jn*. xi, 41.
[4] *Mk*. vii, 34.

[5] *Mk*. ix, 28.
[6] *Mt*. xiv, 19; xv, 36; *Mk*. viii, 6; *Lk*. ix, 16; *Jn*. vi, 11.

Messianic suffering also is signed with the sign of
prayer. St. John, the divine contemplative, has
transmitted to us that great High Priestly prayer in
which Jesus dedicates Himself to His sacrifice, for
the glory of His Father and for the eternal life of
all His disciples.[1] It is with thanksgiving and with
blessing that He institutes the Passover of the New
Covenant in His Blood.[2] In Gethsemane He wins
strength for His Messianic sacrifice by means of
the most intense prayer.[3] And finally, on the
Cross, in the very midst of the agonies of death,
His lips move in the psalmist's prayer: 'My God,
my God, why hast thou forsaken me?'[4] Here
again St. Luke gives us fuller information concerning our Lord's dying prayer. For he tells us how
His redeeming love burst forth even on the Cross
in the appealing prayer: 'Father, forgive them,
for they know not what they do.'[5] And he tells
us also that His last breath was breathed out in
prayer to His Father: 'Father, into thy hands I
commend my spirit.'[6]

If we would understand the prayer of Jesus, we

[1] *Jn.* xvii.
[2] *Mt.* xxvi, 26, *sqq.; Mk.* xiv, 22, *sqq.; Lk.* xxii, 19, *sqq.*
[3] *Mt.* xxvi, 39; *Mk.* xiv, 35; *Lk.* xxii, 43.
[4] *Mt.* xxvii, 46; *Mk.* xv, 34.
[5] *Lk.* xxiii, 34.   [6] *Lk.* xxiii, 46.

20

must explore the mysterious region of His relations with His Father, and we must examine the
character of His teaching.

Jesus was conscious that there existed the closest
communion between Himself and His Father.
'You shall see the heavens opened and the Angels
of God ascending and descending upon the Son of
Man.' [1] This consciousness of interior union with
God was a thing natural to Him, a gladdening
inward reality, constraining Him from His very
boyhood. 'Did you not know that I must be
about my Father's business?' [2] No other word
could express His experience but that word
'Father,' which was so constantly on His lips, and
which He used in such a personal and intimate
fashion. The word, indeed, signifies His peculiar
privilege, for 'no man knoweth the Father but
the Son.' [3] Jesus conjoins Himself and His
Father in a unity in which no other creature can
share. He teaches His disciples when they pray
to say 'Our Father,' for God is the common
Father of all; but for Jesus Himself He is simply
'Father,' 'My Father.' And to Jesus alone comes
the Father's answer: 'Thou art my beloved

[1] *Jn.* i, 52.   [2] *Lk.* ii, 49.
[3] *Mt.* xi, 27; *Lk.* x, 22.

Son.' [1] In that answer His human soul had its deepest and most sublime experience of its mystery, of its profound union with God. For the Son is higher than the angels of heaven.[2] And what Jesus is as the Son, no one knows but the Father.[3] So the prayer of Jesus to His Father is in its deepest ground a constant experience and realization of an essential unity and an absolutely unique Sonship. The Old Testament had proclaimed the great commandment: 'Thou shalt love the Lord thy God with thy whole soul and with all thy strength.' That supreme commandment was never but once understood and obeyed in its whole breadth and depth, and that was by the incarnate Son of God. The prayer of Jesus is the focal point where the vital commerce of His divine and human natures is enacted and fulfilled. When we examine His prayer we are perforce concerned with those mysterious relations upon which the soul of Jesus entered when the Word was made flesh.

Our Lord's prayer sprang from a profoundly personal life, which was the life of a unique personality, at once divine and human. For that reason His prayer was an essentially personal and

[1] *Mk.* i, 11; ix, 6; *cf.* iii, 12; xii, 6; *Mt.* xvi, 16, *sqq.* [2] *Mk.* xiii, 32. [3] *Mt.* xi, 27; *Lk.* x, 22.

inward act. He Himself in vigorous terms condemned verbosity and routine. 'When you are praying speak not much as the heathens do.' [1] A genuine personal experience can take on none but a plain and simple expression. And Jesus forbade everything that might tarnish the purity of prayer, as, for instance, any simultaneous seeking for human praise or purpose of edification. 'And when you pray, you shall not be as the hypocrites, that love to stand and pray in the synagogues and corners of the streets, that they may be seen by men. Amen, I say to you, they have received their reward.' [2] But rather, 'Thou, when thou shalt pray, enter into thy chamber, and having shut the door, pray to thy Father in secret.' [3] According to our Lord's mind, prayer demands a certain naked purity of soul and a removal of all foreign, non-personal elements. Prayer is the meeting of the human personality with the divine, in a great silence where all else is hushed, for God is speaking. Therefore Jesus teaches that prayer is the most personal act that can be conceived, and that an idle, distracted prayer is no prayer at all.

Such pure prayer was unknown before Christ. Hence Heiler can say that the sum-total of what

[1] *Mt.* vi, 7.   [2] *Mt.* vi, 5.   [3] *Mt.* vi, 6.

23

non-Christian religions have to show in this matter of personal prayer is sadly little when compared with the abundance and variety of such prayer in the records of Christianity; and Söderblom, that Christianity is the true home of personal prayer; and Bousset, that it is *par excellence* the religion of prayer.

Our Lord's prayer was an absolutely personal prayer, yet it was also a prayer made in complete union with God, and an activity of His soul within the living God. This profound relation to God was essential to His being. 'My meat is to do the will of him that sent me.' [1] So we may set down this dependence on God as the second characteristic of His prayer. Any private, purely human desires, or choices alien from God, must be banished; a man must lose his life, if he would save it. Nothing counts but the Father's will, both in the accomplishment of good and in the avoidance of evil. 'Hallowed be thy name, Thy kingdom come. Thy will be done on earth as it is in heaven. Give us this day our daily bread. And forgive us our trespasses as we forgive them that trespass against us. And lead us not into temptation. But deliver us from evil.' Of course

[1] *Jn.* iv, 34.

24

the disciple of Jesus will pray for his earthly needs,
for his bread. But even this bread shall be only
his 'daily' bread, bread only for the day. And
both this and whatever else the child may ask from
his Father, must somehow be related to God's
will and to His purpose for the sons of men. Thus
we are left, for the substance of our Lord's prayer,
with nothing but God, His will and His kingdom.
His prayer was a deliberate self-orientation towards
the will of God, an unconditional self-surrender to
Him. But it was not, as in the case of certain
ecstatic natures, a weak, languishing love, nor yet
a love of sweetness and mystic rapture. For
Jesus did not think of God as being utterly apart
from the world, in some remote paradise, accessible
only to the rapture of the disembodied spirit. He
thought of God as very near to the world and as
active in it. 'My Father worketh until now and I
work.' [1] So He found God in the birds of the air
and in the lilies of the field, and His whole attitude
towards nature was a prayer. Above all He found
God in mankind. For men, whether just or unjust,
were children of His Father, for whom He sends
sun and rain. [2] So near does man stand to the
heart of His Father that if we love God we must

[1] *Jn.* v, 17.   [2] *Mt.* v, 45.

also love man, be he Samaritan or Jew, sick or sound, just or sinful. Jesus regards the service of our fellow-men as of the very essence of religion, so that without it there is no true religion. 'And when you shall stand to pray, forgive, if you have aught against any man, that your Father also, who is in heaven, may forgive you your sins.' [1] 'Go first to be reconciled to thy brother, and then come and offer thy gift.' [2] The Pharisee prayed proudly with supercilious contempt of the publican; and therefore the latter 'went down to his house justified rather than the other.' [3] The full, broad stream of pure prayer which Jesus poured out to His Father was transformed into love of man, and came back to the poor and sick and sinful as redeeming and sanctifying power. Not that He was one of those simple enthusiasts who make a religion of the service of humanity; He had no interest in humanity as an end in itself, but in humanity as part and parcel of God's purpose; and regarding man as subject to God's will, He was able to give man a divine value. Nietzsche remarks that in loving man for God's sake, He achieved the most sublime and exalted sentiment that has ever been attained.

[1] *Mk.* xi, 25.   [2] *Mt.* v, 24.   [3] *Lk.* xviii, 14.

Since the prayer of Jesus is thus decisively attached to the active and creative will of His Father, it follows that His prayer is also a practical and resolute service of God, and not an idle complaining or vain desire. It realises actively His own words: 'Not my will but thine be done.'

Here lie the austerity and the heroism of His example. The lesson is a very plain one, and yet so fine and delicate that many have failed in their effort to express it. For the austerity of Jesus does not imply any flight from the world, its riches and pleasures. Nor does it connote that abnegation of which the mystics speak. Nor is it something which we can find in an external consideration of this or that work of His. His austerity and heroism lie in His inward, reverent, strong willing of all that God wills. It is therefore a pure act of the inward man, which is perceptible only to the man himself, and an act which he has constantly to renew, so often in fact as he realises what is the will of God, whether permissive or imperative. So it is, in its outward manifestation, something very simple. And yet, in its inner nature, it is a thing which calls for force. 'The kingdom of heaven suffereth violence, and

27

the violent bear it away.' Nor must we be supposed, in any of this, to imply that God's will—whether permissive or imperative—may be a sort of fate to which man has to resign himself as best he can. There is no question of such weary resignation or passive tolerance of the will of God, but of an active and vital acceptance of it. In the centre of my being I will what God wills, and doing so I will as well every plain, inevitable and unconditional manifestation of His will. This inward affirmation and unconditional acceptance of God's will may be very hard for me, in proportion as His will seems strange and unintelligible, and the less I can discover purpose and wisdom and goodness in it. My task is hardest when I am faced by the evil which God permits. And it is just at this point that the supreme test is made, and my response to that test will show whether the will of God is lord and ruler of my life, so that I am ready for His will's sake to sacrifice even Isaac, my only son. At this point does prayer pass into heroic deed and into that 'violence' which wins the kingdom of heaven, becoming a resolute determination that God shall be all in all. For this reason our Lord's prayer in the Garden of Gethsemane is the supreme type of Christian prayer, and the purest manifestation of its essential character. 'And going a little further he fell upon his face, praying and saying: My Father, if it be possible, let this chalice pass from me. Nevertheless not as I will but as thou.' [1] His Father's will remains for Jesus the supreme and decisive thing, no matter what agony and torture it may bring. As He prayed in the Garden of Gethsemane His soul was seeking amidst its agony for the true will of God, and with 'violence' submitting itself to that will in a perfect 'Thy will be done.'

That scene gives us in the plainest fashion the essence of His Prayer, namely its unconditional acceptance of God's will. His prayer stands on a higher level than any prayer directed to a private and personal end, or one which should seek to traverse or at least to modify the plain will of God. Jesus never asked His Father for any personal favour, and we find Him in His first and second temptations expressly discarding such prayer. His prayer is devoted exclusively to the interests of the kingdom of God, to the glory of His Father. Shortly before His death He prayed: 'Father, the hour is come, glorify thy son'; but even that was for His Father's sake, 'that thy son may glorify

[1] *Mt.* xxvi, 39.

29

thee.' [1] In the hour of extremest peril He refuses to ask His Father to send Him legions of angels.[2]

Nor does Jesus ever ask for the why and wherefore of the divine will. That will is to Him the ultimate and highest reality, the manifestation of the glory of His Father. That a man was born blind, that the Son of Man must suffer: such things are ordained 'in order that the works of God should be made manifest,' and 'in order that the Scripture might be fulfilled.' To ask further questions is not according to the spirit of Jesus.

So since the whole prayer of Jesus is rooted and grounded in the will of God and aims only at the glory and majesty of His Father, it is natural that His prayer should take pre-eminently the form of thanksgiving. He cannot take a piece of bread or fish into His hand, He cannot begin or end a meal without thanksgiving. Before the grave of Lazarus He prays: 'Father, I thank thee that thou hast heard me.' After healing the demoniac of Gerasa He bids him 'Go into thy house to thy friends and tell them how great things the Lord hath done for thee and hath had mercy on thee.' [3] He censures severely the ingratitude of the nine Jewish lepers

[1] *Jn.* xvii, 1.   2 *Mt.* xxvi, 53.
[3] *Mk.* v, 19.

whom He had cured of their leprosy: 'There is no one found to return and give glory to God but this stranger.'[1] At the height of His Messianic activity, when He sees that His work is bearing some fruit in His disciples, His heart is full to overflowing and He breaks forth into fervent thanksgiving: 'At that time Jesus answered and said: I praise thee, Father, Lord of heaven and earth, because thou hast hid these things from the wise and the prudent and hast revealed them to little ones. Yea, Father, for so it hath seemed good in thy sight.'[2]

So far as we have any evidence regarding His prayers of petition, they are related almost exclusively to the glory of His Father and the establishment of His Kingdom. He prays for Peter that his faith may not fail.[3] For His disciples in general He prays: 'Father, I will that where I am, they also whom thou hast given me may be with me.'[4] He asks His Father to send the Holy Spirit, the Comforter, to His bereaved disciples;[5] and He promises to remember His faithful followers when He comes into His kingdom: 'Everyone that shall

[1] *Lk.* xvii, 18. [3] *Lk.* xxii, 32.
[2] *Mt.* xi, 25, 26. [4] *Jn.* xvii, 24.
[5] *Jn.* xiv, 16.

31

confess me before men, I will also confess him before my Father who is in heaven.'[1] And if once in the Garden He begged that the chalice of His bitter Passion might pass away from Him, yet we know that even in that Agony He sought and followed nothing but His Father's will. 'My Father, if it be possible, let this chalice pass from me. Nevertheless, not as I will, but as thou. . . . My Father, if this chalice may not pass away, but I must drink it, thy will be done.'[2]

We may therefore set it down as certain truth that the sole and singular object of our Lord's prayer was the will of His Father. His own human will had no independent rights.

But here is a seeming contradiction. For did not Jesus Himself encourage us when we pray to ask for our personal needs and to tell God confidently of our wishes and desires? 'Ask, and it shall be given unto you'; does it not seem as though we were encouraged to assert our own will? The solution of this question will help us to grasp a further characteristic quality of our Lord's prayer, namely its boundless confidence.

That confidence is part and parcel of His prayer and is inculcated repeatedly in His teaching. Con-

[1] *Mt.* x, 32.   [2] *Mt.* xxvi, 39, 42.

sider the parable of the unjust judge, who grants
the widow's request, not because he fears God or
regards man, but because she is troublesome to
him, and because he is afraid lest continually
coming she should weary him.[1] Consider also
the parable of the importunate friend, who comes
in the middle of the night and knocks insistently,
until the door is opened to him and his request
granted.[2] Consider again the vivid terms in
which he portrays the strength of parental love
and urges full filial confidence: 'What man is
there among you, of whom if his son shall ask
bread, will he reach him a stone? Or if he ask him
a fish, will he reach him a serpent?'[3] And in
many other instructions regarding prayer Jesus
repeats in various forms His encouraging assurance: 'All things whatsoever you shall ask in
prayer, believing, you shall receive.'[4]

This confidence in prayer has never been expressed so boldly, forcibly and unconditionally as
by Jesus. 'I know, Father,' He says, 'that thou
hearest me always.'[5] Nor is it merely that we may
have such confidence when we pray; we *must*

---

[1] *Lk.* xviii, 1-8. [3] *Mt.* vii, 9, 10.
[2] *Lk.* xi, 5-8. [4] *Mt.* xxi, 22.
[5] *Jn.* xi, 42.

have it, if we would ensure the success of our prayer. 'Have faith in God. Amen, I say to you, that whosoever shall say to this mountain, Be thou removed and be cast into the sea, and shall not stagger in his heart, but believe that whatever he saith shall be done: it shall be done unto him. Therefore I say unto you, all things whatsoever you ask when you pray, believe that you shall receive, and they shall come unto you.' [1]

So, according to our Lord's teaching, a firm and unswerving faith that our prayer will be heard is a characteristic of genuine prayer. Nor does He mean that faith itself as a function of the soul and by virtue of auto-suggestion has the power of producing an infallible result. That interpretation of his words is not consistent with His general teaching, nor with His conception of faith, which with Him is always faith in God. Faith is for Him nothing else but a boundless confidence in His Father, to whom all things are possible.[2] Before His omnipotence no natural law may obstinately stand, and it is that same omnipotence that can move mountains.

Thus Jesus bases the omnipotence of prayer

[1] *Mk.* xi, 22; *Mt.* xxi, 21.
[2] *Mk.* x, 27; xii, 24; xiv, 36.

34

confidence and most joyful certitude. 'Let not
your heart be troubled, nor let it be afraid.' Our
Lord's gospel is indeed a *gospel:* it is good tidings
of great joy.

By what way may I come to Jesus and His
gospel? There is one very short and simple way
to Him, and it is this: I look—as we have just
looked—into the soul of Jesus at prayer, and
seeing, I believe.

'Of his fulness we have all received and grace
upon grace.' [1]

[1] *Jn.* i, 16.

CHAPTER III

THROUGH CHRIST OUR LORD

I

It is good for us all at times to pause awhile and to examine our fundamental position, and that not merely from a moral, but also from a doctrinal point of view. In the press of daily life this or that peripheral truth pushes forward into the foreground, so that the central truths are not seen, or not seen in their right perspective. And yet our fundamental attitude is truly Catholic only when we hold the structure of Catholic doctrine in that order and relative proportion in which the Church conceives it and would have it conceived. The Catholic faith is not a mere sum of truths which are strung together in a merely mechanical fashion; it is a living structure of the Holy Spirit, which grows forth out of a living basic principle and develops according to the law of its inner nature. Every truth has its definite place within this living system, its definite function, its organic meaning.

And this is emphatically true of the dogmas which concern Christ.

I should like therefore to speak now about Christ, and in particular about the position which appertains to Christ in our religious life, if we are to be faithful to the directions of dogma. My inquiry is not, 'What think ye of Christ?' for we all gladly confess that He is the Incarnate Son of God, God of God, Light of Light. I am not inquiring into the content of the Christian faith, but only into the position which Christ occupies in the systematic practice of that faith. Is Christ the final and supreme object of our religious endeavour, or must we go beyond Christ to the Father, *per Christum ad Patrem?* In what sense is the Christian's attitude christocentric, and in what sense is it theocentric?

While I endeavour to answer this question I shall assuredly not be expounding any new truth; but the inquiry may nevertheless help to make our faith more lively and definite, more consistent and pure. Much in our faith and in our worship may thereby come into clear light, which hitherto we have not noticed or have noticed only confusedly.

And first let me be allowed to say that the question we are asking is not a purely arbitrary one. Whoever takes note of the course and gentle flow of Catholic piety will observe a varying rhythm in the confession of Christ and a varying emphasis on the sweet and holy Name of Jesus. We may perhaps distinguish two schools of Catholic piety. They are not rigorously separated the one from the other, for they are in contact. And assuredly there is between them no question whatever of any dogmatic difference; for Catholics everywhere believe that Jesus is the Incarnate Son of God and that He is to be adored as God. That faith is the unquestioned basis and root of their Christian life. Nevertheless it may be asserted that this common faith in Christ takes a distinctly different emphasis in the two schools of piety to which I have referred. I mean that there is in this matter a real difference between private and popular piety on the one hand and liturgical piety on the other.

In private devotion the worship of Christ is, speaking generally, so predominant and so much in evidence that faith in the Father and adoration of the Holy Ghost take a notably inferior position. How many are there now who pray to the Father through the Son in the Holy Ghost? And has not the Holy Ghost in particular become for not a few devout people an Unknown God? Is it an exaggeration to say that in popular devotion a recognition of the Holy Trinity survives only in the Sign of the Cross and the Creed? The figure of Christ has so to speak drawn to itself all religious faith and devotion. When we think of God, we think of the glorified Christ. *Omnia ad majorem Christi gloriam.* Christ is our supreme and final goal, and we do not pass beyond Christ to the Father. Thus our worship is expressly christocentric, rather than theocentric. Perhaps we may see a gentle reproof to this attitude in those words of Pope Pius X. in his famous Decree on Frequent Communion (December 20th, 1905)—to which we shall return later—when he lays it down that the primary purpose of the Blessed Eucharist is not *ut Domini honori et venerationi consulatur*, to give honour and reverence to Christ.

And connected with this is the fact that in private devotion several immensely profound and fruitful doctrines of the Faith do not get that position which belongs to them. The more one-sidedly Christ is considered, the more attention is concentrated upon His divinity, and the less He is regarded in His humanity as the 'first-born among many brethren' and the new head of mankind, so

41

much the more do the great truths of His High
Priesthood and His Mystical Body retire into the
background of the devout consciousness. The more
does that lively sense of the union effected by His
grace, of the supernatural fellowship of Christians
in Christ, tend to disappear. The Christian isolates
himself from the Head and from his fellow-mem-
bers in the Body of Christ. He has no feeling of
union and solidarity with Christ and His members,
but a consciousness rather of separation and indi-
viduality. That unity which Paul, Ignatius, Cyprian
and Augustine celebrate over and over again with
enthusiasm as the blessed gift of our salvation,
that *vinculum pacis, spiritus unitatis, unitas carita-
tis,* is no longer, or at least in no sufficient measure,
a regular constituent of Christian sentiment. And
so also the average believer regards the Church
from without rather than from within. He sees
rather its outward hierarchical structure and
imagines that the whole essence of our holy
Church is exhausted in the activities of the priestly
and pastoral ministry, in pope and bishops and
priests. And since he has no lively understanding
of the divine nature of the Church, of the essential
union of all members of the Body with Christ
their Head, and since he does not really feel that

he himself is taken up into the fellowship of the members of Christ, therefore the Church appears to him not as the very basis of his individual life, as the home where he may find his truest life and deepest realization, but rather as something foreign to himself, as a sort of bureau or institution to which he may go if he wants assistance, but which for the rest remains wholly outside the circle of his personal interests, with its own ends, its own methods, its own forms of life. And for this very reason—because the life of the Church has no vital relation to his own life—he is prone to criticize the claims of the Church and to pass judgment on its decisions and decrees as though it were nothing more than an ordinary human institution. And he is only too ready to find its ordinances irksome and disagreeable. He feels the Church as something foreign and forced upon him, just because he has practically lost his feeling of a common fellowship in Christ, and with it the profound conviction that his own supernatural life is to be realized in and with the life of the Church.

But there is another and more awkward consequence of the one-sided prominence given to Christ's divinity and the obscuration of His humanity. In a suggestive essay that appeared not so long ago,[1] Abbot Herwegen of Maria Laach pointed to what he described as an 'enormous change' in the religious attitude during the Middle Ages, a change which began in the Carolingian period and reached its full development in the thirteenth century. The change was this, that the sacramental, objective and social elements of religion receded in favour of the moral and subjective. This change he imputed, at least in part, to the subjective temperament of the Teutonic races, and concluded that their emphasis on moral values and comparative indifference to sacramental and divine causality, resulted in the fashioning of a devotion which relied far more on the personal effort of the individual than on the power of divine grace. In theological language they exalted the *opus operantis* above the *opus operatum*.

Now I confess that I cannot assent to Abbot Herwegen's thesis in its entirety, even in the restricted form in which the revered author, who has done such high service for the liturgical movement, has more recently stated it. But be that as it may, Abbot Herwegen has certainly seen right

[1] *Kirche und Seele, die Seelenhaltung des Mysterienkultes und ihr Wandel im Mittelalter.* Theologische Quartalschrift, 1925, pp. 239, *sqq.*

in this one point, that Catholic piety as practised apart from liturgical worship may foster a state of soul wherein the organic connexion of nature and grace is only loosely held, and where personal activity emancipates itself, so to say, from supernatural influence. But the real basis of this veiled semi-Pelagianism does not lie—as Abbot Herwegen supposes—in a neglect of the sacramental aspect of our religion. It lies deeper than that, in a secret detachment from the Mystical Body of Christ, and deeper still, in the obscuration of belief in the 'first-born' of his brethren, in the Man, Christ Jesus. When the glad consciousness that we have in the sacred humanity of Jesus the sure pledge, guarantee, and most attractive realization of the new life has vanished into the background, or at least grown feeble and vague, then spring up in the impoverished soil of the soul the arid growths of mere morality, and with them all that contorted virtue, extreme asceticism and intense scrupulosity which now and again turn the glad tidings of the gospel into tidings of terror.

That I am not wrong in seeing these connections may be proved if we take a glance at those Christian communities which have removed all human features from the image of Jesus, or at least have not let His substantial likeness with us men stand forth in its full strength and emphasis. I am referring to the Gnostic and Monophysite sects, and in a certain measure also to the schismatical Eastern churches.

The Gnostics explained the humanity of Christ as pure semblance. For them the divinity of Jesus was the sole and proper object of worship. Christ did not redeem us through His humanity, through His passion and death, but through that light of truth flashing forth in His divinity which He sends into our hearts. The consequence was that Gnostic piety had a definitely intellectualist stamp; it was an exercise of thought and reason, and not a loving faith. More than that, it broke up that supernatural fellowship and unity of the Body of Christ which binds the faithful to God and to one another. The Gnostic was the individual *par excellence*. In his creed he had no conception of a mediatorial High Priest, of a Mystical Body of Christ, or of its Head. And for that very reason his notion of the Church was a purely external one. He regarded it, not as a supernatural development and completion of the humanity of Christ unto the fulness of His members and unity of His Mystical Body, but as a merely natural association of like-minded folk, a combination of religious society and philosophical school. So Gnostic piety and morality did not form a life lived in Christ and inspired by the Holy Spirit, but an individual and independent life. Rigidity and artificial exaggeration were native to Gnosticism. In the region of intellect it led to extravagant speculation, in that of will to excessive asceticism. And this latter in the end became so eccentric—at least in Syrian Gnosticism—that it degenerated into a system of caste morality.

Less devastating, but nevertheless critical enough, were the effects on the Monophysite communities and schismatical churches of this same dislocation of dogma and obscuration of the humanity of Christ. Let me cite the witness of Father Joseph Jungmann, S.J., in his substantial and instructive study regarding the place of Christ in liturgical prayer, a book which I shall have much to say about presently.[1] Father Jungmann points out that the Arian heresy, in denying the Son's essential equality with the Father and full divinity, had a remarkable effect, by contrary reaction, on the Eastern liturgies generally. The primitive liturgical formula, 'through Christ our Lord,' and the ancient doxology, 'Glory be to the Father through the Son in the Holy Ghost,' became no longer

[1] *Die Stellung Christi im liturgischen Gebet.* 1925.

tolerable, since the terms 'through Christ,' 'through the Son,' could be interpreted in an Arian sense as implying the inferiority of Christ, and were in fact so interpreted by the Arians. Therefore St. Basil the Great and St. Athanasius also replaced the ancient formula: 'Glory be to the Father through the Son in the Holy Ghost' either with 'Glory be to the Father with the Son and with the Holy Ghost,' or with 'Glory be to the Father and to the Son and to the Holy Ghost.' The ancient expression of Christ's mediatorial function, 'through the Son,' was abandoned. So, too, we find St. John Chrysostom changing 'through Him' into 'with Him.' And he alters the so-called 'grace formula,' which originally was an appeal to the Father to grant our prayer through the merits of His Son, into the form 'May the grace of our Lord Jesus Christ move the Father to give us His gifts.' In Monophysite circles this form obtained exclusive supremacy, and the original form came to be regarded as heretical.

How did these liturgical alterations affect the religious attitude of the people who used the new formulas? In all these churches the sense of the importance of Christ's humanity in our redemption faded. In the Monophysite churches it perished utterly. Fulgentius observes that Eutyches, the founder of the Monophysite heresy, had no longer any place left for the priesthood of Christ in his doctrinal system. In the non-moniphysite Greek and Russian churches also, the designation of Jesus as our High Priest—so frequent in the liturgical language of the first centuries—became ever more and more rare. And this involved a complete revolution in christology. For now Christ no longer stands by man's side, as the representative and advocate of mankind, and no longer as the man, Christ Jesus, and the First-born of His brethren, offers the sacrifice of mankind to the Triune God. He has, so to speak, crossed over, and is now by God's side, and Himself is the awful and unapproachable God. He has become infinitely remote from men, and in the Eucharist itself He is regarded as the infinitely exalted God who perfects the mystery. As Jungmann says,[1] the memory of the God-Man who instituted the sacrifice is overlaid by the thought of the divine Presence. Jesus is now the divine consecrator who effects the holy sacrifice. The thought of His divinity engulfs all else in the liturgy, and the priest becomes no more than a shadow of the Son of God. The result was

[1] *Stellung*, p. 214.

on the one hand, from the time of the Emperor Justin II. (565-578), the gorgeous development of the liturgy, and on the other hand, a complete transformation of the religious attitude. It is significant that this transformation set in with the very theologian, St. John Chrysostom, who first regularly corrected 'through Him' into 'with Him,' and first therefore exchanged the soterio-logical outlook for the trinitarian. Characteristic of this attitude is that sense of an immense distance between us and the divine Presence in the Eucharist, leading to boundless reverence and even to fear and awe. Now for the first time in the history of the Eucharist is there talk of the 'awful sacrifice,' of the 'awful bread,' and of the 'fear and trembling' with which we should receive the Body of the Lord. Up to the fourth century such expres-sions were unknown. The adjectives 'terrible,' 'fearful,' 'dreadful,' 'awful' now for the first time make their appearance in eucharistic literature. Religion from a religion of love has become a religion of fear. And in order to give outward expression to the new sense of remoteness from the eucharistic God, the altar is withdrawn from the gaze of the people, first by means of curtains, and later by the painted wooden

partition of the iconostasis. The eucharistic
sacrifice has come to be regarded as essentially the
awful mystery, and if it still preserves something
of the attractiveness of mystery, that element is
only faintly discernible. The faithful felt themselves faced by an infinitely awful reality, the
stupendous fact that God immolates Himself for
man. For the first time there now appeared the
notion of the eucharistic slaying, from which
notion were derived the later, post-Tridentine
destruction theories. Faced with this awful reality,
the faithful found no support or comfort in their
own human world, no refuge in a holy humanity
which being unspotted by sin could stand before
God to intercede for the brethren and reconcile
the world with Him. There was no longer a
living faith in the Man Christ, the first-born among
the brethren, the new Adam. Thus they were
dominated by a feeling of boundless guilt, nor
could this feeling find any genuine relief through
trust in the Man Jesus, through any assurance of
safety here and now by union with Him in His
Mystical Body. This feeling of guilt held the faithful back from the altar. It is instructive to note
that St. John Chrysostom is the first bishop who
has to complain: 'We stand idle round the altar;

there is none who partakes.[1] Out of this feeling
of guilt, moreover, grew those self-accusations,
those repeated self-reproaches of the priest and
faithful in Holy Mass, which we meet especially in
the Gallican liturgies. The Gallican and Spanish
liturgies underwent the same process of alteration
as the Eastern liturgies and for the same reason.
The Arianism of the Visigoths attacked the pure
divinity of Christ, and so these liturgies were
altered in an anti-Arian direction to insist on that
divinity. The primitive formula 'through Christ'
was replaced by 'through Thee, God.' And here
also it was not the Man Jesus who was the High
Priest, but the divine Christ, our God. And so here
also the fundamental religious attitude was one
of awesome fear and scrupulous self-accusation.
St. Paul had said: 'Let a man prove himself,
and so let him eat of that bread,'[2] prescribing
such self-examination as a preparation for the
celebration of the Eucharist. But now (especially
from the ninth to the eleventh century) it was
vastly overdone, and was introduced into the
liturgy itself, continually interrupting the prayers.
Only with the eleventh century were these
self-accusations which had overgrown the whole

---

[1] *Hom.* xvii, *in Heb.,* 4.   [2] *I. Cor.* xi, 28.

liturgy gradually discarded. Our *Confiteor* at the beginning of Holy Mass is but a tiny remnant of them.

Let me now very briefly indicate another process that went on in the schismatical churches, parallel with the weakening of belief in the humanity of our Lord. This was the development to an extreme point of the veneration of the saints. For in those churches the saints now separated themselves, so to speak, from the mediatorship of Christ—which had become obscured—and asserted their independence. According to the conception of early Christianity, as that has remained dominant in the Roman Church, the saints are members of the Body of Christ. Certainly they are its most distinguished and valuable members, whose intercession has especial power with Christ; but they remain always its members. Whatever they do, they do it only through Him; and they form along with the rest of the faithful a single society of the redeemed, a single fellowship living in Christ. Their intercession is not different in kind from the intercession of any member of the Church. They belong to the Church, even if, being its most distinguished and holiest members, their intercession is of more effect with God than the intercession of other

members. And so the Church, turning to Christ
for grace, takes the saints with her in her prayer.
The saints were and are dependent upon Christ
and live through Him alone. When the Church
takes them with her in her prayer, her intention
simply is that their intercession should strengthen
the prayer which the *Ecclesia orans,* the whole
praying Church, makes with them to Christ.[1] This
conception of the function of the saints still domi-
nates the prayers of the Roman Mass.

But where the other tendency has prevailed,
where men have forgotten the High Priesthood of
Christ and removed the High Priest Himself away
from contact with mankind, relegating Him to the
infinite sphere of the divine, there it was inevitable
that this conception of the function of the saints
should disappear. For there was left, in such a
religious belief, a yawning gulf between man and
the purely divine Christ, and the saints were
naturally called in to bridge this gulf. Thus they
take the place of Christ as intercessor of the praying community. And so in the later form of the
Byzantine liturgy the invocation of the saints, the
appeal to their intercession, is a regular conclusion
of solemn prayer, just as the phrase *Per Christum*

[1] Jungmann, *Stellung,* p. 240.

Dominum nostrum is in the Roman liturgy.[1] Hence came a certain extravagance in the veneration of the saints as practised in the Eastern churches. The great truth, to which St. Paul testifies so often, that 'Head and Body are one Christ' was not indeed denied, but it was in serious danger of being obscured; for certainly, it was not profoundly realized.

I need scarcely point out expressly how this new religious attitude, deriving from the struggle with Arianism and resulting in an undervaluation of the humanity of Jesus, has influenced the whole spiritual make-up of the Eastern Christian, and in particular of the Russian. For Christians of the West the same influence had no very lasting opportunity of making itself felt, for the Gallican and Spanish liturgies, which had been transformed by the anti-Arian trend, were ultimately absorbed by the Roman liturgy. We shall presently hear how the Roman liturgy is the only one among all Christian liturgies that declined to revise its liturgical prayers in the struggle against Arian error. Men speak of the Russian, of his passive temper and gift for self-surrender, of his self-depreciation and utter indifference in regard to earthly interests,

[1] Jungmann, *Stellung,* p. 237.

and at the same time of the basis of his attitude, namely his vivid eschatological hope. They will tell you of his constantly recurring delusion that the Son of Man must come in the next generation, of his passionate longing for resurrection and a new life, and of his exaggerated veneration of the saints. It is not hard to recognize that special circumstances and definite historical experiences have had an important share in the development of this type. But the decisive influence has been the liturgy, and especially the anti-Arian conception of Christ which the liturgy held constantly before his eyes. Wherever the devout soul has its gaze fixed exclusively on the divine Christ and contemplates only the dread God who is slain for the sins of mankind, wherever it forgets the 'first-born among many brethren' and no longer realizes that it has already in this life, in and through this First-born, a genuine fellowship with all the saints, a Church and a home: there the devout soul is compelled to put its trust more and more exclusively in the world to come. For the undervaluation of the humanity of Christ necessarily brings with it an undervaluation of everything human and earthly. And then in effect there remains for us in this world nothing but that stern command that

56

came of old to the monk Arsenius: 'Flee, be silent, weep.'

Thus our examination of Gnosticism and of Eastern and Russian piety has revealed to us all those characteristics and consequences which we believe necessarily arise for the religious attitude of the faithful when the humanity of Jesus is obscured. And therefore there stands before us once more in plain evidence the ancient truth, that dogma is the very structure of life and that it can endure no sort of obscuration or curtailment. Only where it can work in unweakened strength and purity do there arise men, spiritualities, saints, having in them nothing warped or distorted, but formed in all things according to the measure of Christ.

And where is it that dogma can exert its power in all its strength and purity? We answer that it can do so in that sphere wherein the infallible and only true Church reveals her supernatural consciousness in the most intimate and tender fashion, where she breathes forth her faith spontaneously in prayer. It is that second sphere of which we spoke at the beginning of this chapter and which we distinguished from the sphere of private devotion, namely the sphere of liturgical prayer.

II

It is not the least merit of Jungmann's book that he has proved that the Roman liturgy alone remained unaffected by the dogmatic struggle of the fourth century. Nor that the Roman liturgy passed entirely unscathed through that severe contest which the Church had to wage with Arianism; for there are, here and there, indubitable traces of the struggle. But it is none the less true that the Roman liturgy is distinguished among all others for its fidelity to the ancient forms. In none is the thought of Christ our Mediator, that is to say, the High Priestly function of the humanity of Jesus, so powerfully expressed. That is a point which I need not establish in detail. The Church concludes no prayer without the decisive clause: 'Through Christ our Lord.' In the Prefaces of the Mass Jesus Christ is represented either as the ultimate ground of the thanksgiving or as its mediator. The first words of the Canon assert His mediatorial function: 'We humbly beseech and pray Thee, most merciful Father, through Jesus Christ Thy Son.' These very words of the Canon go to prove that the liturgical formula 'Through Christ our Lord' is not to be restricted to the sense

58

of 'through the merits of Christ' as won for us by
the sacrifice of Calvary, but connotes also that
High Priestly activity of Christ whereby He is continually offering our prayers to the Father, 'always
living to make intercession for us.' [1] Consequently at the present day in the Roman liturgy,
and in it alone, is that law still effective which was
formulated at the Synod of Hippo in the year 393
and in the presence of St. Augustine. The twenty-
first canon of that Synod lays it down that the
prayers of the liturgy should be addressed always
to the Father: *Semper ad Patrem dirigatur
oratio.* We are instructed to pray, not to Christ,
but through Christ to the Father, through God
Incarnate to the Triune God.

This liturgical rule is in entire harmony with
dogma, for it corresponds with what revelation
teaches us of the fundamental relations existing
between God, Christ and the Church.

Certainly, according to revelation, Christ is the
Second Person of the Blessed Trinity and true God.
As the Creed says, He is God of God and Light of
Light. But He is also true Man, consubstantial not
only with the Father, but also with us. Jesus has
a purely human consciousness, a purely human

[1] *Heb.* vii, 25.

will, a purely human emotional life. He is a complete man. So unimpaired is this human nature of His that its union with the divine Word is founded only upon the unity of the (divine) Person, and implies no destruction of itself. The mystery of the Incarnation does not necessarily entail any communication of the divine nature or attributes to the humanity of Christ. On the contrary, that humanity persists, even after its union with the Word of God, in its specifically human quality. The Second Person of the Blessed Trinity, the Word of God, contributes nothing to the human nature that implies any enrichment of the human nature as such. What is contributed is simply the Person. Without here investigating in detail the character of this personal union, we may nevertheless say this much: that it involves such an intimate and essential conjunction of the human nature with the divine Word that this nature belongs essentially to the divine Word, that it is His humanity, and that the divine Word can say, 'I am this man.'

And therein lies the mystery and the miracle of Christ. It is not that a human nature was taken up into the divinity, but that the divinity became a full and perfect man. It is not the ascent of the human to the divine, but the condescension of the divine to the human. It is not that flesh became God, but that God became flesh. Such is the mystery, the miracle, the stupendous prodigy. And hence the thrill and the joy of those words: 'And the Word was made flesh.' Can we utter them without thankfulness and joy? 'He emptied himself, taking the form of a servant, being made in the likeness of men, and in habit found as a man.' [1]

Why is the Incarnation the fundamental and decisive thing? Because it was the first manifestation and the literal bodying forth of God's will to redeem mankind. There is no conceivable form of redemption in which God's love could have revealed itself so visibly, so forcibly, so effectively as in the Incarnation. So visibly: for what is more visible than flesh and blood, more visible than the Child in the manger, than the Crucified, than the Risen Christ? So forcibly: for what more could God have done than give us His only-begotten Son? And so effectively: for when God became Man, the redemption was no longer a mere announcement of glad tidings of future joy; it was already a present joy and a resplendent reality. We had a new Man in our midst, one who might

[1] *Phil.* ii, 7.

61

with pure heart cry 'Abba, Father,' and to whom there came the heavenly answer: 'Thou art my beloved Son.' The many thousand generations of mankind, separated from God in their first parent, were again at this one point united to God, and so firmly and essentially united with Him that there shall never again be separation. In this One Man the whole of humanity was raised from out of its nothingness and worthlessness, and given a positive being and a genuine worth. And since this elevation of mankind was a fundamental and a real elevation, therefore were we made a genuine and a real unity in Him. He is our new foundation, our new origin, our new root. We are related to Him as the branches are to the vine. He is the Head of the Body, and we are the members. There is really now no longer any individual or isolated man, for we are all members of Christ and He is our Head. As there is but one Head, so is there but one Body.

And that is the central point of the glad tidings of the gospel. The vital fact is not that God dwelt bodily among us and that we can see the glory of God in the face of Christ Jesus, but that this God is our brother, that He is of one blood with us, that He is the Head of our body. Of course, the divinity is an essential element in the picture of Christ. If Christ were not true God, then the infinite gulf between God and the creature would not be bridged in the Person of Jesus. That was the point of the fierce struggle with the Arians. That struggle drew its energy and fervour from this very conviction, that if Christ be not Himself true God, He cannot raise us to God and give us to share in the divine life. But this divine element is not the only element in the picture of Jesus; nor is it even the prominent element, during the time of this world. Rather it is the golden background, from which His human activity stands out and from which it draws its secret strength and redeeming power. It is the element of peace and repose. But contrasting with that quiet setting is a thrilling fact: this divinity appearing in our human form. Incredible though it may seem, we have among us a man who is God; in His Person all mankind is formed into a unity and bound to God; and we all through Him have access to God. For that is the deepest meaning of Christ to us, that we go through Him to the Father. The vital fact for us and for our world is not that He as the Incarnate God is entitled to the adoration of men, but that as the New Man He makes all who would be saved

members of His body and as King of God's new
people leads them to His Father. Parallel with
the eschatological contrast between this world and
the next, between seed-time and harvest, there is a
christological contrast between the Man Christ
Jesus here and the Triune God there, between the
Kingship of the Incarnate here and the rule of the
pure Godhead there. There is a deep meaning in
the statement that the history of Christianity is the
history of the becoming, unfolding and realization
of the man Christ Jesus. In the doctrinal, priestly
and pastoral functions of the Church the glorified
Christ prosecutes His Messianic work. In that
same Church He builds Himself His body. As
St. Paul says, the Church is His fulness.[1] Through
her He becomes whole and complete. For as long
as His Father wills that this world shall endure,
for so long is Christ unfinished and incomplete.
He is still ever at His work, still constantly acting
as our mediator. Continually, in all places and at
all times, he is completing Himself in ever new
members, until according to God's unsearchable
decision the Last Judgment shall come and the new
era be inaugurated. Then end the eschatological
and christological contrasts of which we have

[1] *Eph.* i, 23.

spoken. The time of Christ's becoming and ripening, the time of His redemptive, mediatorial, high-priestly activity terminates; and the time of the Triune God begins. Then will He as the Head of the Body, as the King of the new Israel, lead His people to His Father and resign His authority to the Triune God: 'And when all things shall be subdued unto him, then the Son also himself shall be subject unto him that put all things under him, that God may be all in all.'[1]

I need not show you in detail how plainly the New Testament evidence concerning the devotion of the early Christians to our Lord supports these fundamental ideas. We know that Jesus, while He lived on this earth, directed all His prayers to the Father. He never requires His disciples to adore Him. What He does require of them is that they should pray to the Father in His Name, that is to say in faithful union with Him. True, He once speaks of prayer to Himself, and promises His disciples that He will grant what they ask Him.[2] So that prayer to Jesus is permitted, and He is the proper object of adoring worship, not only as the Word of God, but also as God made Man. But,

[1] *I. Cor.* xv, 28.   [2] *Jn.* xiv, 14.

for the period of this world, while requiring men to recognize his Godhead, He desires that in their worship they should regard Him as their Mediator. Certainly we know that the early Christians prayed to Jesus, not merely in petition,[1] but also in praise;[2] but these prayers either are concerned expressly with His redeeming function, or else occur only in private devotion. In its solemn prayer the early Church turned to the Father, to the Triune God;[3] yet of course that prayer was quickened and supported by the thought of Jesus and by the consciousness of union with Him. The Christian confessed Jesus in his baptism, celebrated the memory of His death in the breaking of bread, and implored His coming in his prayers: 'Maranatha, Come, Lord Jesus!' It was always Jesus round whom his thought revolved, but the goal of his prayer, with Jesus and through Jesus, was the Lord God. Hence the primitive Christian formula of prayer: 'in the name of Jesus.' 'Giving thanks always for all things, in the name of our Lord Jesus Christ, to God and the Father.'[4] 'All whatsoever you do in word or in work, all things do ye in the name of the Lord Jesus Christ, giving thanks to

[1] *Acts*, vii, 59. [2] *Apoc.* v, 13; vii, 10; xi, 15.
[3] *Acts*, iv, 24; xii, 5. [4] *Eph.* v, 20.

God and the Father by him.' ¹ It is practically
equivalent to that other formula: 'through Jesus.'
St. Peter writes: 'that in all things God may be
honoured through Jesus Christ.' ² St. Paul: 'I
give thanks to my God through Jesus Christ.' ³
St. Paul even seems to indicate that this formula—
'through Jesus'—had already taken its place in the
apostolic liturgy.⁴

This manner of prayer was a direct consequence
of the apostolic teaching regarding the mediatorship of Christ. There was no truth which the
Apostles strove more strongly to impress upon their
disciples than this one: 'There is one God, and
one mediator of God and men, the man Christ
Jesus: who gave himself a redemption for all.' ⁵
'We have an advocate with the Father, Jesus Christ
the just, and he is the propitiation for our sins; and
not for ours only, but also for those of the whole
world.' ⁶ The *Epistle to the Hebrews* employs the
language of liturgy and describes this mediatorial
activity of Jesus as a high-priestly activity, setting
the Son of God before our eyes as the Eternal High
Priest: 'Having therefore a great high priest that

¹ *Col.* iii, 17.
² *I. Peter,* iv, 11.
³ *Rom.* i, 8; xvi, 27, *etc.*
⁴ *II. Cor.* i, 20.
⁵ *I. Tim.* ii, 5.
⁶ *I. Jn.* ii, 2.

hath passed into the heavens, Jesus the Son of God, let us hold fast our confession. For we have not a high priest who cannot have compassion on our infirmities, but one tempted in all things like as we are, without sin.'[1] And the early Church held fast to this apostolic teaching regarding our High Priest. It was so dear to it that up to the end of the second century the Church abstained from applying the title *priest* to its ministers, lest it should be misunderstood by Jews and pagans. Up to the fourth century all liturgical prayers were directed to the Father through this High Priest. The formula, 'through Jesus Christ thy Son,' found as early as the *Didache,* which is the most ancient Christian writing outside the New Testament, recurs in all the early Christian liturgies without variation, except that it develops either into the formula 'through Jesus Christ in the Holy Ghost,' [2] or—inasmuch as the Holy Ghost works in the Church—into 'through Jesus Christ in the holy Church.' [3] Only towards the end of the fourth century was this sacred rule violated, so that there crept into the liturgy from private devotion forms of prayer that were addressed directly to

[1] *Heb.* iv, 14.   [2] *Cf. Eph.* ii, 18.
[3] Hippolytus.

Christ. To be sure these prayers are in the beginning found only in the ante-mass and in the ritual of baptism, and never in the eucharistic service. It was the anti-Arian struggle—as has been pointed out already—that first brought this new mode of prayer into the innermost sanctuary.

The fact that the Roman Church remained substantially true to the ancient tradition gives its liturgy its pre-eminence, and proclaims once again the consoling truth that it, and it alone, not only in its faith, but also in its prayer, is inspired by the Holy Spirit. It is true that there are in its liturgy a few prayers which do not conform to the ancient rule, but are addressed to Christ alone. Under Pope St. Gregory the Great the *Kyrie eleison* was taken over from the book known as the *Apostolical Constitutions*. Later on the praises of the *Gloria* were addressed to the Son as well as to the Father, and the *Benedictus qui venit* was added to the *Sanctus*. Pope Sergius I. took over the triple *Agnus Dei* from anti-Arian sources. And the three prayers to Christ before the priest's communion were added at a very much later date. There are besides a couple of prayers in Advent deriving from the Gallican liturgy, and the prayer for the feast of Corpus Christi. But, even so, all these prayers bear the soteriological stamp, for their object is our Lord in His character of Saviour and Redeemer, and not purely in His Godhead. They are directed to the Lamb of God, our Mediator; and by the constantly recurring 'through Christ our Lord' they are all worked into the texture of that ancient prayer, whereby the Mass is in a supreme sense 'the sacrifice of our Mediator.' [1]

If then we desire to pray according to the mind of our Lord and the manner of the early Christians and the will of the Church, we can do so by following the liturgy and by praying 'through Christ our Lord.' That is the profound value of the liturgical movement of our days, that it is revealing once more the rich significance of the liturgical formulas and that it is teaching us to assimilate our own practice to the spirit of the liturgy.

And what is the significance of the formula 'through Christ our Lord'? In the first place, and before all else, it teaches us that we are most intimately united with Christ our Head, and brings home to us the fundamental fact that as Christians we live and move in Christ. Within that general effect we may distinguish two particular results of this teaching. The one is that we get a vivid

[1] St. Augustine, *Enchiridion*, 110.

70

realization of our native remoteness from God and of our natural inability to reach God by our own power, so that we are substantially grounded in the fundamental Christian temper of humility, and being true fellows of the humble publican reject and discard all presumptuous self-confidence. The other result is that we get a joyful certainty that in Christ we have all. This is the high mood of Christianity, the holy joy of the redeemed, who can no more despair for their sins, whose whole life now is centred, not in the struggle with sin, but in love for Christ. Christianity is joy, Christianity is trust, Christianity is constant thanksgiving. How much good will has already been squandered to no profit, because we insist on setting our own strength between us and Christ, because we would work out our salvation through ourselves, and because, even when we utter the words, we are not really living and praying 'through Christ our Lord'!

But the third value of those words for us is certainly the least appreciated of all. We mean the lesson that St. Paul inculcates when he insists that 'Head and Body are one Christ.'[1] Here is the widest gulf between our piety and that of the early Church. How vividly did the Christians of the

[1] *I. Cor.* xii, 12, *etc.*

71

early centuries realize the truth—and how deeply they were penetrated by it—that they in Christ their Head were united and formed into a new supernatural unity, a spiritual temple, a chosen generation, a royal priesthood, a holy nation.[1] There are few doctrines which from the very start were proclaimed with such confidence, clarity and fervour as was the truth of the mystical unity of the faithful in Christ and of their holy priesthood. So real was the supernatural mystery of the Church to those early Christians, that the Gnostic heretics took the conception of the 'heavenly Church' and gave it an independent existence as a spiritual entity. In its relation to God the early Church was a supernatural fellowship, a community solidly compacted in Christ, and not a congeries of isolated individuals. It was only later, in conflict with the heretics who denied that the Church was one and visible, that the structural form that Christ Himself had imposed upon His Church was fully realized and formulated in exact theological language. Then was the official priesthood distinguished precisely from the priesthood of the laity, and the bishop distinguished from the priest. But, even so, the supernatural and invisible unity of the Church

[1] *I. Peter* ii, 5-9.

remained throughout axiomatic and unquestioned. It is not till the Reformation period, when Lutheran theology exaggerated the priesthood of the laity, that Catholic apologists here and there seem in the stress of the conflict to have lost sight of that principle, and to have formulated an unduly empirical and external notion of the Church. But in the beginning it was not so. The Christian regarded his Church from within and not from without. He regarded it primarily as a Body whose Head is Christ. And that selfsame conception of the Church remains to our own day presupposed in the prayers of the liturgy.

Indeed, it is the truest and deepest meaning of the liturgy; this is my last point, and it seems to me the most important. The communion with the flesh and blood of Christ which we celebrate in the liturgy is a real communion with Christ our Head, and therefore a real communion with all His members. 'For we, being mañy, are one bread, one body, all that partake of one bread.' [1] This aspect of the Eucharist is emphasized by St. Paul, and especially by such Fathers as St. Ignatius of Antioch, St. Cyprian and St. Augustine. Their constant teaching is that by means of this one

[1] *I. Cor.* x, 17.

heavenly Bread the supernatural unity of the many in Christ is established and realized. The Mass is never an individual act, but always essentially a community act; and this not merely in the sense that the whole community should take part in it, but also and emphatically in the sense that participation in the one Bread gives the community its true cohesion and unity, and builds it up into the supernatural organism of the Body of Christ, in which form it is presented to the Father by the hand of the divine High Priest. The ultimate meaning of Holy Communion is not union with the uncreated Word, with the pure Godhead, as some ancient Greek theologians erroneously held; nor is it more than a half-truth to say that its meaning is union with the living Christ. The full truth is that it is union with Christ and through Christ with all His members, in whom, in mysterious yet real manner, He achieves His fulness. The Eucharist is not the sacrament of the personal Christ alone; it is also at the same time and for that very reason the sacrament of the mystical Christ. It is a community thing through and through. This truth has long been an accepted fact among the historians of dogma, nor can the Fathers be understood if we ignore it. And now it has been confirmed by the historians of the liturgy, such as Jungmann and Kramp. Jungmann lays stress on the fact that the liturgy still represents the Eucharist, not as an end in itself and an object of worship, but as a means to an end, that is, as a sacrament; for it represents the Eucharist as a sacrificial gift and then as the sacrificial food of the community, which shall unite them to one another and form them into the Body of Christ. The personal presence of Christ in the Blessed Eucharist is a certainty of our faith, but the liturgy does not dwell upon that presence, or seek to adore it, lest it should obscure the proper purpose of the sacrificial food, which is communion. The liturgy turns to the glorified Christ and through Him begs the Father that He would not deny to 'these holy mysteries,' the sacrament of the flesh and blood of Christ, their proper 'fruit,' which is nothing else than the communion of the faithful in Christ. For —so Jungmann declares—'it is precisely this communion and fellowship, the normal condition of the living Christian, that the sacrament is intended to secure.' [1]

Whatever part of the liturgy we examine, we find Christ represented as our Head who binds us

[1] *Stellung,* p. 227.

together into one whole and offers us with thanksgiving to His Father. We are continually brought back to that fundamental attitude which is indicated in the ancient formula 'through Christ our Lord.'

It is none of my business to inquire whether we have actually in our current practice exhausted the immense possibilities of this substantial prayer, or have not rather dug for ourselves various trivial and paltry cisterns, although we had in our dogma and in our liturgy rich wells of the water of life. Yet I wonder if we are not ourselves responsible for the fact that in many regions of devotional life there seems to be little appreciation of the inmost treasure of Christianity, of its truest glory and strength. Has not that Christianity, which we plant and water, become variously a weary, wilted morose Christianity, and not a victorious and glad Christianity? Do we Catholics really feel and realize that holy unity and sacred fellowship whose Head is Christ, or are we not isolated and separated one from another, forming all too often no more than an external organization? I see but one road to renewal, and that is the road which both dogma and liturgy point out to us, and of which we ourselves shall be daily reminded, as often as we pray 'through Christ our Lord.'

CHAPTER IV

CHRIST'S REDEEMING WORD

WHEN we read St. Matthew's Gospel it immediately becomes plain to us that Jesus regarded His preaching as a substantial part of His redemptive work and looked upon Himself as eminently a teacher. In His first sermon, in the synagogue at Nazareth,[1] He preached from a passage in the prophet Isaias which emphasized this teaching office of the redeemer: 'the spirit of the Lord is upon me, wherefore he hath anointed me, to preach the gospel to the poor.'[2] He laid express claim to the honourable title of Master: 'You call me Master and Lord, and you say well, for so I am.'[3] He claimed the title in an exclusive fashion: 'Neither be ye called masters; for one is your Master, Christ.'[4]

Humanly speaking we may say that the quality above all others which gave His preaching its power was its originality; He had not got His

[1] *Lk.* iv, 18.
[2] *Is.* lxi, 1.
[3] *Jn.* xiii, 13.
[4] *Mt.* xxiii, 10.

doctrine from another; He had not, like St. Paul,
sat at the feet of any Gamaliel. He had been
brought up as a carpenter, in what we should call
working-class conditions, nor had the means of
human culture been accessible to him. We hear
nothing of any teacher of His, and His own towns-
folk were amazed at His preaching: 'How came
this man by this wisdom? Is not this the carpenter's son?' [1] What He gave the people was
His own, and not learnt from another: 'I speak
that which I have seen with my Father.' [2] The
sole book that He constantly cites is the Holy
Scriptures, the written word of His Father. Jesus
lives and moves in the language, imagery and
thought of the Old Testament; but He uses the
Old Testament, not as the devout scholar or humble disciple, but as the Lord and Master who has
come to fulfil its every word. He quite deliberately
sets His own word against the word of Moses and
the old dispensation: 'It was said to them of old
. . . but I say to you.' [3] The Old Testament has
for Him no supreme and final authority, for He
Himself, the Incarnate God, is that authority.
Hence His independent judgments and His setting

[1] *Mt.* xiii, 54. [2] *Jn.* viii, 38.
[3] *Mt.* v, 21.

aside the authority even of Moses. Even when He
is expounding sacred Scripture, He is independent
of it, remaining wholly Himself in mind and will.
That was true of Him when He stood in the Temple as a boy of twelve, and they were all 'astonished
at his wisdom and his answers.' [1] And when in
that same Temple at the prime of His life He proclaimed His new Gospel to the Doctors of the Law,
they cried out in utter amazement: 'How doth this
man know letters, having never learnt'; [2] so completely different was His manner of reading and
interpreting the Scriptures from the manner of the
Scribes. The people were quickly alive to the
difference: 'They were astonished at his doctrine,
for he was teaching them as one having power,
and not as the Scribes.' [3] A greater than they, and
a greater than Moses had now come, one who
had not to make laborious search for truth, but
already possessed it in Himself, in His own immediate experience. He had but to dip into the rich
treasure of His own mind in order, as He expresses
it, to bring forth new things and old. [4]

His preaching is so exceedingly simple, yet at
the same time so forcible, just because it is based on

[1] *Lk.* ii, 47.
[2] *Jn.* vii, 15.
[3] *Mk.* i, 22.
[4] *Mt.* xiii, 52.

this immediate experience and personal knowledge. It is characteristic of Him that He says the most striking and arresting things in so simple and natural a way that they seem inevitable. 'Martha, Martha, thou art careful and art troubled about many things. But one thing is necessary.' [1] That sentence, uttered with such effortless ease, has shaped countless lives, drawing men from worldliness and distraction to a sublime life of the spirit. Or what shall we say of those words to the sinner: 'Many sins are forgiven her because she hath loved much'? [2] Have they not illumined with their radiance many a forlorn and dismal life, and directed innumerable souls to triumphant sacrifice and self-surrender? 'Unless ye become as little children, you shall not enter into the kingdom of heaven': how many have been rescued by those words from a proud and self-satisfied culture, and brought back to simpleness and humble duty? We might go on thus interminably, examining each saying of our Lord's in the light of its tremendous influence. 'Give to Caesar the things that are Caesar's and to God the things that are God's.' 'What doth it profit a man if he gain the whole world and suffer the loss of his own soul?' 'He

[1] *Lk.* x, 41.   [2] *Lk.* vii, 47.

80

that loses his life shall save it.' There is nothing rhetorical about these sayings, nor any striving after effect. The language of the prophets was far more vigorous and more loaded with imagery. It was alive with personal passion and glowed with a holy wrath. But the language of Jesus is quiet, simple, homely, and natural, like Himself and like those children whom He loves so much. There is, it is true, a hint of Jeremias in His words when He has to condemn the Pharisees or confute the Scribes; but for the rest His language is fragrant of the lilies and olive-trees amid which it was uttered, and we can hear the birds singing. And yet, for all their simplicity, His words are eternal, and as fresh now as when they were first spoken. Time cannot impair them, for, as the simple fisherman Peter recognized, they are the words of eternal life.[1]

Our Lord in His preaching showed a predilection for two literary forms, the proverb and the parable. His proverbs are concise, clear and to the point, and consequently they imprint themselves indelibly on the memory. Sometimes they are cast in the form of paradox, as in 'He that loseth his life shall save it.' His sentences are as a burning flame or a two-edged sword. 'If thy eye scandal-

[1] *Jn.* vi, 69.

81

ize thee, cut it out.' They are short and sharp, like
a sudden blow or the crack of a whip. 'If a man
strike thee on thy right cheek, turn to him also the
other.' 'Love your enemies, do good to them that
hate you.' Nor have these sentences lost anything
of their vivid force and power to sway the hearts
of men.

The other form which He employs to convey
His teaching is the parable. His parables are
among the most beautiful things in the literature
of the world. They are so profound and pregnant,
that the learned man cannot exhaust their meaning, and on the other hand so simple and unaffected as to captivate the poor and the uneducated.

Sometimes, it is true, He is more technical
employing the scriptural argument which was in
vogue among the rabbis, as when He reminds the
Sadducees, who denied the resurrection, of the
words of *Exodus:* 'I am the God of Abraham, and
the God of Isaac, and the God of Jacob.' [1] Again,
in controversy with the Pharisees, he uses *Psalm*
cix.: 'The Lord said to my Lord,' and to prove
that the Messias cannot be the offspring of David
in the natural sense, and is not of earthly origin. [2]
But even in using this scriptural argument He dis-

[1] *Mk.* xii, 26.   [2] *Mt.* xxii, 41.

dains the apparatus of learning and refrains from wordiness. His conclusion emerges from the text as something self-evident, and it is this very self-evidence which confounds His opponents.

Such easy, effortless greatness is characteristic of the divine; while laboured argument and ramshackle theory betray the hand of man. When the truth flashes into our sight with meteoric radiance, and in its naked beauty dazzles our eyes yet holds them with its loveliness, we may recognize the work of God. Truth is always simple and quiet, for it is always its own sufficient evidence. We read [1] that Elias, having zealously fought for God's law for many years, fled into the wilderness and sought a sign of the divine presence. There came a strong and mighty wind; but the Lord was not in the wind. After the wind came an earthquake and after that a fire; but the Lord was not in earthquake or in fire. And then there came the whistling of a gentle air, and Elias wrapped his face in his mantle and stood in the door of the cave and listened, and God spoke to him in that gentle stillness. So was it with the voice and word of Jesus. His preaching had that quality of gentleness and quiet, of stillness and limpid clarity,

[1] *III. Kings* xix, 10.

which belongs to the voice of God and the word
of eternal truth.

Jesus is, therefore, the wonder of the world: in
the intellectual sphere, for 'never man did speak
like this man';[1] and also in the moral sphere, by
reason of His radiant sanctity. For He not only
taught as one having authority; He also lived
according to His teaching; He asked nothing from
others that He did not Himself perform; He practised what he preached. St. Luke says of Him,
very significantly, that 'Jesus began to do and to
teach,'[2] setting performance before precept. And
that is the way of the genuine teacher of men,
himself first doing that thing which He would
teach others. Our Lord's teaching was the direct
expression of His life and personality, and in this
point He surpasses other teachers of mankind,
who have propounded systems of life and then
neglected to follow their own teaching. For this
reason, as Voltaire remarked, no philosopher has
ever converted so much as the street in which he
lived. Jesus taught what He had Himself willed
to do, and with Him to will was to be able. In
His death He was the great teacher of the art of
dying, teaching us the hardest lesson of all and

[1] *Jn.* viii, 46.   [2] *Acts*, i, 1.

one wherein the teacher must himself die. Since
Calvary we have known that death is the way to
life.

We have had much to say about the characteristic manner of our Lord's preaching; let us now
speak about its substance. And first we ask this
question: Did He do nothing more than present
old truths in a new and attractive form, or did He
bring new truth to men and thereby make them
free? Our answer is that His teaching was in an
eminent degree original and new.

In the first place we may say, in quite general
terms, that it was His most conspicuous achievement and singular triumph to have proclaimed
God to the world in the most perfect fashion. He
taught two truths about God which revolutionized
religion: His utter supremacy and His fatherhood.
Let us take these in order.

Jesus presented the Lord God as without question or rival the last end of man, as the deepest
and ultimate meaning of life. As a consequence
He taught men to regard the service of God as the
one great business of life, the one thing necessary.
We Christians have become so used to this conception of God, that it seems to us obvious and
self-evident, and we do not realize the originality

of our Lord's teaching. Yet it is true, none the less, that He was the first to open men's eyes to the truth, and the first to teach men what God truly is and what their service should be.

There is no need to remind the reader how distorted was the idea of God before Christ came. Polytheism with its multitude of gods and goddesses, demigods and tutelary spirits, had confused and destroyed in men's minds the conception of a transcendent God of infinite perfection and sanctity. Even in those religions, such as the Babylonian, Persian and Chinese, in which the service of God had a definitely ethical character, there was no pure conception of His nature. Speaking generally, the service of God was regarded as a business transaction: *do ut des*. Man offered God his moral obedience and religious worship, and God in return gave man long life and prosperity and like benefits. God, so to say, existed for man, and not man for God. Nor were things much different in Judaism, although the prophets had over and over again insisted on the sublimity of God; for practical piety laid itself out to do a profitable business with God and degraded the infinite Deity into a servant of human selfishness. The concepts of reward and punishment, merit and demerit, dis-

torted by this selfishness, were central concepts of
Jewish piety. It was supposed that God did not
regard the disposition and intention of His wor-
shipper, but only the work and service which He
tendered; and that He rewarded those precise
services with a definite earthly recompense, a reim-
bursement in the earthly currency of health and
wealth and abundance of children. Religion was
no longer, so to say, the free daughter of heaven,
but the handmaid of covetousness and elaborate
self-seeking. In the time of our Lord this sort of
piety was especially developed among the Pharisees, and Jesus delineates it well in His satirical
picture of the Pharisee who went up to the temple
to pray, but spent his time in a pompous enumera-
tion of his good works: 'I fast twice in the week; I
give tithes of all that I possess.' [1] The Pharisee
supposes that God will make haste to reward
these services with their appropriate recompense.

It is our Lord's great achievement that He
utterly destroyed this unworthy idea of God.
Proclaiming the unsearchable mystery and unapproachable majesty of God, He revealed something
of the rich life of Father, Son and Holy Spirit in
the eternal commerce of the Blessed Trinity. Such

[1] *Lk.* xviii, 9.

a God had no need of creatures, but creatures certainly needed Him; so much so that God is the very life and value and meaning of their lives. In this way our Lord reversed the current religious attitude by putting God at the centre and teaching that He does not exist for man, but man for Him. In doing this He also revolutionized morality, for He made enthusiasm possible, and detachment from the world and self, and desire of the infinite Good, and love of the Eternal. A modern philosopher, Oswald, has complained that his monistic morality cannot produce or foster any heroic virtue; and what else is to be expected, if *natural* law conditions and determines every act and all its consequences? Unselfishness and heroism are only possible when the agent has before him a value which is infinite, which is wholly above creatures and exempt from all their limitations. He has then a supreme good which invites his whole interest, strains all his powers, and by its service makes him free. The fine flower of pure goodness and genuine unselfishness—without which no virtue is really virtue—is possible only when a man sets before him as his end not a mere earthly ideal, but simply and singly the infinite Majesty of God. Nietzsche has said that when a man ceases to find greatness in God, he ceases to find it anywhere. When our Lord taught men that God was the Supreme Good of the universe He then first made possible that true morality, which consists in doing good for the sake of the Good.

Most impressive, and for the novice in the faith even disconcerting and alarming, is the emphasis with which our Lord over and over again sets forth God and God alone as the true and pre-eminent goal of all our desire and all our doing. He declares that His business, and the business of all men, is to co-operate in the fulfilment of God's will in the world. This is the one pearl of the Kingdom of Heaven, the one treasure found in the field, for which we must give up everything else.[1] In that marvellous prayer which He taught His disciples and in which He expressed in matchless fashion all that lay near to His heart, all the desire and hope of His soul—the *Our Father*—He begins in the very bosom of eternity with 'Hallowed be Thy name; Thy kingdom come; Thy will be done on earth as it is in heaven.' His dearest delight is that God, the Life of His life, should be glorified, His kingdom established, His will performed. That prayer at once with a mighty wrench jerks

[1] *Mt.* xiii, 44.

89

us free from the earth and its limitations, and carries us to God.

We may therefore say that His special redemptive achievement, so far as His teaching is concerned, was that He delivered religion from a merely natural orientation and from the grip of purely natural aims, in order to reveal its true supernatural character. He showed that God was not the mere henchman of man, but Himself His own end and the end of all being. And thus morality was delivered from earthliness and set free from its preoccupation with personal advantage. Thus a truly free, unselfish and heroic striving was made possible.

This exposition of the nature of God and of true religion is therefore the great achievement of Jesus in His character of teacher. It is a lesson which has in it an austerity and rigour which make it formidable to the natural man. For if God is all this and man must give Him so unconditional a service, then he must with equal absoluteness deny his own purely natural being. To love this great God he must hate his own life.

But this austerity and rigour are transfigured, our hearts are reassured and gladdened, by means of the second correction which our Lord made in the current conception of God, namely His teaching that God is our Father. It is true that God had already received that title among many primitive and savage peoples, for the history of religion has provided abundant evidence of the fact. There are peoples who while professing belief in various special deities and spirits and practising magical rites, yet have a certain faith in a supreme Father, to whom they offer no sacrifice, but who is tacitly honoured as the giver of all good, conserver of the world, and future rewarder. Yet this belief, such as it is, is so overwhelmed by their superstitions and polytheistic practices that it is practically stifled. Among the Greeks and Romans there was also this conception of God as Father (Zeus, Jupiter), and the later Stoics liked to use the word *Father* of the principle which they made responsible for the order of the world. In the Old Testament God is several times called Father, as for instance by the prophet Jeremias when he compares the goodness of Jahwe to Israel with the love of a father for his children, and encourages the people to call upon the Lord as on their Father: 'Call to me: "Thou art my father."' [1]

So God was already known as our Father in the

[1] *Jer.* iii, 4, 14, 19.

pre-Christian period, but He was very rarely so addressed by the heathen. Nor was He called Father in the full meaning of that word by any people of those times, even by the Jews. Jewish piety in the time of our Lord regarded God as the Holy One, that is to say as something remote and awe-inspiring. They believed that they could not serve him better than by fulfilling in fear and trembling, and down to the last iota, the law which He had given to Moses. Not only so, but they had to obey the multitudinous and multifarious regulations whereby the rabbis had applied the law to daily life. The natural result was a vast externalization of piety. Religion came to mean the exact performance of the most trivial actions according to the prescribed ritual, and the whole religious life, thus constricted in the strait-jacket of legalism, was turned into a tedious obedience and a mere doing of certain specified works. The fundamental disposition, both in Jewish and in pagan religion, was fear: amid the Jews, fear of the dread Judge and jealous Guardian of the law; amid the pagans, fear of the envy and anger of their deities. Until we contrast our Lord's teaching with these religions of fear, and in particular with the petty narrowness and oppressive legalism of

92

Jewish piety, we shall not fully appreciate the novelty of His gospel.

God is not in His fundamental nature the rigid guardian of righteousness, exclusively occupied in securing the observance of His commandments. He is not an Attorney-General with all His attention directed towards the administration of law. Nor is He a Chief Rabbi whose business is to see that the legal rules are correctly applied to the smallest details of life. He is none of these things; He is our Father. He is concerned not only with dead law, but also with living men. He does not regard law and doctrine as ends in themselves, but as instruments subservient to the higher purpose of guiding poor erring man to His Father. And the same is true of every earthly chastisement and penalty. Such things are not ends in themselves; they are means which our Father uses in order to keep us in the right path. For His great purpose is the healing of the sick soul, and the rescue of the lost. 'They that are whole need not the physician, but they that are sick.' [1] An earthly father will not disown his son, so long as that son still bears some love towards him; but our heavenly Father is infinitely better than any earthly father.

[1] *Lk.* v, 31.

The earthly father will not give his son a stone when he asks for bread, or a serpent when he asks for fish, or a scorpion when he asks for an egg.[1] 'How much more will your Father who is in heaven give good things to them that ask him?' [2] Such is the fundamental nature of God—His absolute goodness. God is love.[3] God is our Father. Jesus proclaimed this redemptive gospel with force and vigour unparalleled. He bade us, when we pray, think first of the fatherhood of God: 'So shall ye pray: Our Father, who art in heaven.'

Therefore the basic disposition of the new Christian piety is no longer, as in the Old Covenant, fear of God, but a childlike love for our Father. The Old Testament commandment: 'Thou shalt love the Lord thy God with thy whole heart' is no longer just one of the six hundred and thirteen commandments enumerated by the rabbis, but the supreme commandment. Our Lord awakened in mankind a new and passionate emotion, the feeling of childlike love for our heavenly Father.

And with that feeling towards our Father there came an entirely new moral disposition. For if God be our Father then we owe Him not merely the formality of external acts, but also the inten-

[1] *Lk.* xi, 12.   [2] *Mt.* vii, 11.   [3] *I. Jn.* iv, 15.

tion of our hearts. And so this principle of inward disposition became fundamental to Christian piety, and the piety of the Pharisee was absolutely and finally rejected. The decisive thing now is not what a man does for God, but how he does it. The poor widow, giving only a farthing, gave more than all the rest.[1] And look at those other types of this new piety: the publican, turning from sin to God and with a full heart crying, 'Lord, be merciful to me a sinner'; the prodigal coming back to his father, with his 'Father, I have sinned against heaven and before thee: I am not now worthy to be called thy son'; the 'woman that was in the city, a sinner' who washed the Lord's feet with her tears, and to whom many sins were forgiven because she loved much; and the little children who turned to Him with pure hearts and trustful eyes, and whom He set before us as our model, 'for of such is the Kingdom of Heaven.'

This then was the revolution that Jesus worked by His teaching of the Fatherhood of God. He altered the whole religious outlook of mankind and created a new race of men, of men with childlike love and simple faith and purity of heart. 'Blessed

[1] *Lk.* xxi, 3.

95

are the clean of heart, for they shall see God.'
Indeed the whole of that supreme Sermon on the
Mount is a delineation of the essential character-
istics of this new creation, the Christian man.

But Jesus, the great divine Teacher, did not only
discover God to men; it is His further redemptive
achievement that He revealed the mystery of man.
From Jesus we first learnt what man is in himself,
and what we men are for one another.

And first, what man is in himself, a knowledge
that was utterly hidden from the ancient world.
For in the great despotisms of the ancient East the
ruler alone was truly and fully a man. Upon him
all other men depended for their existence and for
the conditions of that existence; before his supreme
power there was no such thing as personal rights
or individual values. And in the ancient republics
of Greece and Rome, the life of the individual citizen was wholly subordinated to the interests of the
city-state, apart from which it had no substance
or significance. This collectivist conception of
human existence is to be found also in the Old
Testament. In the most ancient period the heads
of the great families, the patriarchs, were the true
subjects of right, or legal persons; the members of
their families were merely objects of right, little

better than chattels. Later on the place of the patriarchs was taken by the kings, who exercised an absolute authority, with the critical preaching of the prophets in some measure counterbalancing and mitigating their absolutism. So also in the Old Testament it is not the individual Israelite who enjoys the privileges of the Covenant, but the people of Israel or their king. It is not till close on the time of our Lord's coming that we discern any traces of a personal faith and a personal piety. In our Lord's time the true heirs of the kings of Israel were the propertied classes of the Sadducees and Pharisees, and these classes had exclusive possession of human rights, in contrast with the unprivileged masses of the poor and lowly. To these poor, disinherited folk belonged also the 'sinners,' by which was meant not people who were far from God, but people estranged from the law, who in the stress of life and daily toil could not find time and opportunity to fulfil every tittle of the law in the manner of Pharisees. Indeed, poverty itself was taken as indicating God's displeasure and marking a certain outlawry; for God would never allow His elect, the genuine sons of Israel, to suffer such want, and wealth was the special sign of His approval.

Thus in the time of our Lord, the full rights of human personality were awarded only to the select few, and were denied to all others. That was the case throughout the ancient world, among the Jews as among pagans. The later Stoics, it is true, reasserted human rights and gave them a theoretical formulization. The Roman Empire, with its union of so many peoples in one vast organization, had the effect in philosophical speculation of reducing the importance of what was merely national, and of bringing into prominence what was human and universal. Stoicism taught that all men have citizen rights in the world, and it is significant that among the teachers of this doctrine were an Emperor (Marcus Aurelius) and a slave (Epictetus). But the Stoic doctrine remained in the region of theory, and did not pass as an enkindling and awakening force into practical life. If we inquire what was the chief reason of this failure, we must find it in the fact that the Stoics based their teaching regarding human rights upon the cold abstraction of natural law, and it remained mere theory and mere words. They did not base those rights on a religious foundation, or anchor them in the eternal, immutable and ever active will of the living God. And there is this further reason for their fail-

ure. The ideal of stoicism was the production of
the 'wise' man—the man who acts without passion
purely in accordance with the dictates of reason.
This aim tended to the formation of an aristocracy
of intellect and to the severance of the proud
philosopher from the ignorant herd, so that the
doctrine of the equal human rights of every
individual necessarily remained an abstract theory.
Seneca, for instance, is eloquent on the full human
rights of the slave and yet cannot refrain from
comparing a slave with a watchdog and encouraging us to regard them similarly. We find also that
the sons of the family are to be educated, but not
the slaves. We conclude that the Stoics, and especially the later Stoics, certainly maintained the
theory of the equal human rights of all men, but
they neither based this theory on a religious foundation, nor urged it greatly, nor propagated it
among the masses. Their theory was the offspring
of effete speculation and was devoid of the fresh
force of life. It was undoubtedly one of the noblest
products of ancient thought, but it was born in the
decay of the ancient world and was itself lacking
in youth and vitality.

To reveal the full meaning of man it was necessary that a stronger than they should come, and

that stronger was Jesus. He taught the infinite value of man's soul, that he is called to the Kingdom of Heaven, that he is the child of God. He represented the poor and the persecuted, the beggar and the mourner, the feeble and the blind and the lame, as all gathered together, from the highways and byways of the world, to the blessed marriage-feast. And not least of all He displayed in His own person the marvel of God made man surrendering Himself to suffering and to death for all men. By such teaching and such example He destroyed the very basis of all exclusiveness and caste, for He established each individual human being as true personality, set him free from all social, economic or political bondage, and gave him an independent value and independent rights. Jesus taught that redemption was for the individual man and his immortal soul, and that there was nothing whatever on earth that was more valuable than a man's soul. 'What doth it profit a man if he gain the whole world and suffer the loss of his own soul?' By attributing to the human soul an eternal destiny, by relating it to the redeeming purpose of God, and by Himself laying down His life for it, Jesus gave the human soul an absolute importance and a supernatural value. So high indeed does man stand in the purpose of God that God Himself sacrificed His human life for him.

In teaching the infinite value of the human soul Jesus taught us at the same time what should be our relations one to another. For if every soul is of infinite value and beyond all price, then it follows necessarily that we must love all men, that we must have the love of our neighbour. Each soul of man is equal in value to every other soul and we are all neighbours. We are all brothers and sisters, children of the same Father, disciples of the same Saviour, friends of the same God. It is true that the Stoics, too, taught such a universal love, and that general benevolence is a central requirement of Buddhist ethics. But the Stoic doctrine, as we have seen, remained mere ineffective theory, for it was a product of philosophical thinking and not inspired by the driving-force of the living God. And the benevolence of Buddhism is a purely negative thing consisting in freedom from any evil disposition. Their doctrine is that a positive activity of love or hate, like every active doing, strengthens the desire for existence and hinders our complete extinction and passing into nirvana. Consequently Buddhist benevolence is not love, but only a refusal to be involved in any positive passion; and therefore it is essentially selfish in its nature. The first real teacher of a genuine love of mankind was our Lord. The love that He taught was a noble and generous and chivalrous love: 'If a man constrain thee to go one mile with him, go with him other two.'[1] It was an unselfish love: 'If you salute your brethren only, what do you more than others? Do not also the heathens do this?'[2] It was an active, keen and practical love. The Stoics had cast their golden rule into the negative form: 'Do not to another what you would not that another should do to you.' Jesus changed this into the positive command: 'All things therefore whatsoever ye would that men should do to you, do you also to them.'[3] In the parable of the Good Samaritan He gives incomparable expression to His conception of true neighbourly love. And as with His teaching in regard to the infinite value of man's soul, so also with this active love of mankind: Jesus bases it on a religious foundation and in that way secures its vitality and fruitfulness. That is the most important respect in which His teaching regarding this love is distinct, not only from pagan teaching, but also from the teaching of the Old Testament. The

[1] *Mt.* v, 41.   [2] *Mt.* v, 47.   [3] *Mt.* vii, 12.

102

Old Testament had already formulated the commandment of love in the words: 'Thou shalt love thy neighbour as thyself'; [1] but, like that other commandment, 'Thou shalt love the Lord thy God with thy whole heart,' it was only one among very many others. It was not set forth as a principal commandment, nor was it conjoined in an inward organic unity with the supreme commandment of the love of God. Jesus was the first to insist on this unity. 'The second is like to this: Thou shalt love thy neighbour as thyself.' [2] 'All things therefore whatsoever ye would that men should do to you, do you also to them. For this is the law and the prophets.' [3] According to Jesus, the love of man is a practical application of the love of God. We cannot really love God, if we do not love man, His child and image. We cannot serve God if we violate our duty towards our neighbour. The service of love ranks above the observance of the Sabbath; for the Sabbath is for man, and not man for the Sabbath. [4] Reconciliation with our brother takes precedence of sacrifice: 'Go first to be reconciled with thy brother, and then coming thou shalt offer thy gift.' [5]

[1] *Lev.* xix, 19.   [2] *Mt.* xxii, 39.   [3] *Mt.* vii, 12.
[4] *Mk.* ii, 27.   [5] *Mt.* v, 24.

The care of our parents is more important than gifts to the priests.[1] In loving men we love God; our love of men is a religious act, a service of Jesus. 'As long as you did it to one of these my least brethren, you did it to me.'[2] Therefore religion and morality, the love of God and love of our neighbour, are not two distinct things which may—as with the Pharisees—come into direct opposition; they are only different aspects of one and the same love.

And when He gave the love of men this religious foundation our Lord at the same time made it a universal and catholic love. If we are to love men for God's sake, then we must love all men, for God is the common Father of all. In the new love, therefore, there will be no anxious questioning regarding relationship, social status, nationality, religion. In the parable of the Good Samaritan our Lord discards such considerations, showing us a true love which was quite independent of them. And He would even have us silence our moral repugnances. For He Himself was a 'friend of publicans and sinners';[3] He spoke kindly to the harlot,[4] and refrained from condemning the

[1] *Mt.* xxiii, 14; xv, 4.　　[3] *Mt.* xi, 19.
[2] *Mt.* xxv, 40.　　[4] *Lk.* vii, 37, *sqq.*

adulteress.[1] The parables of the strayed sheep, of
the lost groat, of the prodigal son, are all intended
to soften our hearts, to fill them with kindliness
towards the sinner, to guard them against all
prudery. There is nothing in the whole world
which should hold us aloof from man, not even
their sins. And so Jesus is not afraid to ask from us
the very highest measure of love for our fellow
man: 'Love your enemies, do good to them that
hate you, pray for them that persecute and calum-
niate you: that you may be the children of your
Father who is in heaven.' [2] Could there be a more
sublime love than this? Here we see clearly revealed the superhuman and supernatural character
of Christian love. When He bids us love our
enemies, Jesus expresses in the purest fashion His
entirely novel way of regarding men and their
solidarity. And since the natural man would find
this commandment hard to understand and still
harder to practise, our Divine Teacher Himself
first lived it in His own person: 'Father, forgive
them, for they know not what they do.' [3] He
gave us no more profound or more moving in-
struction than that, from the sacred pulpit of His
Cross. There is concentrated all the luminous

[1] *Jn.* viii, 1, *sqq.*   [2] *Mt.* v, 44, 45.   [3] *Lk.* xxiii, 34.

105

teaching of the Light of the World regarding man's nature and man's love. And there also is the source and origin of His own redeeming love. 'The Son of Man is come not to be ministered unto but to minister, and to give his life a redemption for many.' [1] In laying down His life for us, He became the master of ministering love. Calvary is the luminous fulfilment of all that He had said and required in regard to love.

Such therefore are the redeeming truths contained in the preaching of Jesus: that the Triune God is the true and sole meaning of my life, and that God is my Father; that my soul has an infinite value; that my love for God should be manifested in love for my fellow men. By this teaching Jesus unveiled for us the mystery of our relations to God and to man, but not that mystery only, for His teaching illumined the impenetrable darkness of that ultimate and most painful mystery, which to the natural man is an insoluble riddle, the mystery of suffering and death.

If God is the end of my life and if God is my Father, then suffering and death cannot be the grim operation of demonic forces, or the pitiless product

[1] *Mt.* xx, 28.

of immutable natural law, or the consequence of personal guilt. Suffering should be regarded rather, in its universality and inevitableness, as an expression of the will of God, that is of the will of our Father. No single sparrow falls to the ground without the Father's will.[1] But where the will of the Father is, there must also His blessing and His help be. Thus suffering and death can no longer signify hopeless evil and unrelieved gloom. Whatever may befall, the Father's will is there and the end must be blessing. And suffering has this great function, that it tests and purifies our love. Suffering *tests* my love and tells me whether I am truly seeking God alone without selfish ulterior motives. Suffering *purifies* my love, because it softens my hard heart, so that my soul the more easily escapes from its selfish bondage to seek the Father alone. That is why Jesus chants the canticle of the Cross, and why He utters those significant beatitudes: 'Blessed are the poor; blessed are they that mourn; blessed are they that suffer persecution.' If we would follow Him, there is nothing for it but to bear the Cross. 'He that taketh not up his cross and followeth me, is not worthy of me.'[2] The Cross is an essential element in true Christianity.

[1] *Mt.* x, 29.   [2] *Mt.* x, 38.

From this time forth the law of life is happiness amid sorrow and tears. In the Cross is life, in the Cross is strength, in the Cross is joy of soul. Suffering is not punishment, or fate, or divine envy. It is a blessing and a genuine source of the love of God. In this way our Lord's teaching transfigured suffering, and doing so changed the whole outlook of the Christian man. If suffering comes from our Father, then it loses all its sting. A distinguished surgeon has observed that the Christian is helped to bear physical pain far better by the strength of his faith than by the doctor's opiates. Faith can overcome all pain, because it sees the blessing in pain. And in order that His disciples might fully realize the blessing of pain, our Lord Himself drank the chalice of suffering to the dregs, a chalice full of physical and mental agony. From His Cross there streams a heavenly radiance, a golden light, upon all those thousands of sick and dying who daily climb the hill of Calvary. It is calculated that of some fifteen hundred millions of living men, thirty millions die every year, which means about fifty-seven every minute—so that every second sees a man die. So death is not a rare and extraordinary thing, but a thing that is happening every day and hour and moment. Our life is a constant dying. The ancients were terrified by the inescapable nature of death; but Jesus banished that terror. For death is no longer the power that plunges the torch of our life to extinction, but one that makes it shine more brightly for eternal life. How brightly shone the torch of life over Calvary when those words were uttered: 'It is consummated!' Let the sick man open his eyes to this divine light, and he will see himself on the royal road of the Cross, and will know that beyond his Golgotha too will come the gladness of the Resurrection. How many millions of Christians have already passed along this royal road! It is from Christ the divine Teacher of living, suffering and dying, that came that heroic courage which in so many saints directly challenged suffering and rejoiced in it. For Jesus is our Teacher of living, but also of suffering and of dying. And indeed He is our pre-eminent Teacher of living just because He has taught us to suffer and to die; for these also belong to a complete life. Here lies the last and deepest characteristic of His teaching, that He taught us not only about the brilliant surface of life but also about its gloomy depths, its suffering and its mortality.

In such ways as these is our Lord's teaching

truly redemptive. He redeems us from bondage to nature, and sets our thinking and willing free for heavenly matters. In the first place, He makes us see God as He is, in that supreme majesty which engulfs all earthly interests, and in that fatherly goodness which draws forth the best that is in us. Secondly, He makes us see man as he is, as the possessor of an immortal soul and as one who is conjoined with us in an equal fellowship in God. And thirdly He reveals the mystery of suffering and death, and shows their hidden power of blessing.

So is He verily the great, the holy, the redeeming Teacher of Men.

'Neither be ye called masters: for one is your master, Christ.'

CHAPTER V

CHRIST'S REDEEMING WORK

IF we reflect upon our Lord's attitude towards man and His redemption, we may on a superficial view run up against a contradiction. For, on the one hand, our Lord certainly regarded man as in a bad moral state, and on the other, He as certainly expected from him the most sublime virtue: 'Be ye perfect, even as your heavenly Father is perfect.' On the surface there is a contradiction here, a conflict between a pessimistic and an optimistic view of mankind. Let us examine this apparent contradiction, and so seek to come to a better understanding of our Lord's teaching regarding our redemption.

In taking a pessimistic view of our moral condition our Lord was in agreement with the devout folk of His time, who indulged in such views to the point of despair. At an earlier period the prophets had painted the sinfulness both of Jew and Gentile in the most dismal colours. Penance and conversion were the two main topics of their

111

preaching; but they did not expect a conclusive conversion until the Messianic period. 'Behold the days shall come, saith the Lord, and I will make a covenant with the house of Israel, and with the house of Juda. . . . This shall be the covenant that I will make with the house of Israel after those days, saith the Lord. I will give my law in their bowels, and I will write it in their heart: and I will be their God and they shall be my people.' [1] Micheas, Isaias, Zacharias and Daniel all express themselves similarly. The greater were the national tribulations, the deeper and more general became this conviction of sinfulness, and the louder the call to repentance. In the latest period this consciousness of sin often degenerated into despair. And it was the best characters who were especially afflicted with despair, and convinced of the hopeless uncertainty of salvation. In the apocalypse of Esdras we meet with some extreme expressions of that despairing anxiety. 'It were better the earth had never brought forth Adam.' [2]

It is in the light of this general moral uneasiness that we can best understand St. John the Baptist's preaching of the gospel of repentance. His baptism, the evangelist tells us, was a 'baptism of

[1] *Jer*. xxxi, 31, 33.   [2] *IV. Esdras* vii, 46.

penance unto remission of sins.' [1] In his eyes the whole people, and not only certain sections of them, were steeped in sin. And he warned them vehemently not to be heedless of his message because they were children of Abraham.

Some liberal theologians would have us believe that Jesus did not share the Baptist's views, but was distinguished on the contrary by the optimism of His outlook. They maintain that His charm and His power were directly due to His optimism, and that, as the sun disperses the mist, His cheerful faith banished anxiety and conviction of sin, restoring confidence and hope of forgiveness. There is a modicum of truth in this statement of the case, which we shall consider later; but for the present we note that it ignores a fundamental fact when it supposes that Jesus did not regard human nature as warped and depraved. The fact is that He attributes to it a definite inclination towards evil, and on that ground regards all men as sinners, and none as exempt from the general condemnation. It is true that He speaks as though some men were just and some free from the sickness of sin, when He says: 'They that are in health need not the physician, but they that are ill'; and,

[1] *Mk.* i, 4.

'I am not come to call the just, but sinners.' [1] But
He spoke those words in ironical answer to the
Pharisees, who regarded themselves as just. If we
want His real opinion of them and their virtue,
expressed unequivocally, we may find it in the
parable of the two sons, [2] in the parable of the
Pharisee and the publican, [3] and in His vigorous
denunciation of Pharisaic ways. [4] Certainly He
would seem to attribute a considerable degree of
perfection to His disciples, for He speaks of them
as the 'friends of the bridegroom,' 'sons of light,'
the 'salt of the earth,' and the 'light of the world.'
But when He speaks of them so, He is thinking of
their future activity as redeemed and elect souls.
In respect of their own nature in itself and of
itself, they are as much under sin as the rest of
men. Once He turned on Peter himself and called
him Satan; [5] and to all the disciples He had to say
sorrowfully: 'O incredulous generation, how long
shall I be with you? how long shall I suffer
you?' [6] The evangelists repeatedly reveal the fact
that the apostles were not fully capable of understanding Jesus, and they show them to us, on the

[1] *Mt.* ix, 12, 13.
[2] *Mt.* xxi, 28-30.
[3] *Lk.* xviii, 10-14.
[4] *Mt.* xxiii.
[5] *Mt.* xvi, 23.
[6] *Mk.* ix, 18.

114

very eve of His return to His Father, quarrelling about questions of precedence.

Jesus was not blind to the meanness and misery of our poor humanity. He told His hearers to their faces that they were 'evil,' a 'generation of vipers,' an 'evil and adulterous generation.' [1] Therefore the first thing that he had to say to mankind was 'Do penance.' [2] And His first act was to accept the baptism of John, and so do vicarious penance for the sins of men. John was for refusing to baptize Him, because such a baptism implied the forgiveness of sin; [3] but Jesus, though knowing Himself pure of all sin, yet would submit to it, 'so that all justice may be fulfilled.' For the sake of this 'justice' He would enter into the sins of the people and take them upon Himself. And His Father's word confirmed and requited His humble self-surrender: 'Thou art my beloved Son; in thee I am well pleased.' [4]

His subsequent preaching also is dominated by the thought that all men are under sin. 'Then began he to upbraid the cities, wherein were done the most of his miracles, for that they had not done penance. Woe to thee, Corozain; woe to thee,

[1] *Mt.* vii, 11, 34, 39.   [3] *Mk.* i, 4.
[2] *Mt.* iv, 17.   [4] *Mk.* i, 11.

Bethsaida.' [1] In the parable of the rich man and Lazarus He would seem to express a darker pessimism in regard to the wealthy and comfortable, who will not listen to Moses and the prophets. 'Neither will they believe if one rise again from the dead.' [2] When eighteen Galileans were killed by the collapse of a tower in Siloe, He asked: 'Think you that they also were debtors above all the men that dwelt in Jerusalem? No, I say to you; but, except you do penance, you shall all likewise perish,' [3] which implied that all Jerusalem was guilty. And those that claim the title of 'just are especially guilty, since they refuse to recognize their moral condition, whereas harlots and publicans recognize theirs and do penance. 'For John came to you in the way of justice and you did not believe him; but the publicans and the harlots believed him. But you seeing it did not even afterwards repent, that you might believe him.' [4] Therefore, sin being so prevalent, 'the Son of Man is come to seek and to save that which was lost,' that is to say, the whole sinful world. [5] And His disciples, when they went forth from Him, 'preached that men should do penance.' [6]

[1] *Mt.* xi, 20.　　[2] *Lk.* xvi, 31.　　[3] *Lk.* xiii, 5.
[4] *Mt.* xxi, 32.　　[5] *Lk.* xix, 10.　　[6] *Mk.* vi, 12.

116

CHRIST'S REDEEMING WORK

So Jesus was no exponent of a cheerful optimism in regard to the moral condition of men. His insight was too clear and Himself personally too pure, for Him not to realize the general wickedness and depravity of the world.

And yet the same Jesus expects from this depraved humanity the most sublime virtue. 'Unless your justice abound more than that of the Scribes and Pharisees, you shall not enter into the kingdom of heaven.' [1] Nor is the new justice to be better merely in comparison with the justice of the Scribes and Pharisees; it is to be perfect justice conforming to an absolute standard. 'Be you therefore perfect, as also your heavenly Father is perfect.' [2] The new justice excludes not only evil actions, but also bad thoughts and angry feelings. It requires us to love our enemies, not merely as a counsel of perfection, but as a moral duty. Worldly solicitude and the attempt to serve both God and mammon are condemned as heathen conduct. The whole inward man must belong to God and His will. 'Thou shalt love the Lord thy God with thy whole heart, and with thy whole soul, and with thy whole mind. This is the greatest and the first commandment. And the second

[1] *Mt.* v, 20.   [2] *Mt.* v, 48.

117

is like to this: Thou shalt love thy neighbour as
thyself.' [1] In all these commandments it is not a
question of a single heroic act which anyone might
be able to produce at a pinch, but of a permanent
righteous disposition out of which good actions
naturally grow, as good fruit from a good tree.[2]

How is our Lord able to make these severe
demands upon us and to promise eternal happiness
to those who fulfil them, if all men are 'evil,' if we
are 'an evil and adulterous generation?' Should
we not rather despair of heaven and with the
disciples ask, 'Who then can be saved?'[3] Here
again is our difficulty.

We can solve this apparent contradiction only if
we take account of our Lord's twofold nature and
of the consciousness which was his in virtue of his
twofold nature. When He speaks in such severe
terms of the sinfulness of men, He is looking at
the world around Him and painting it in its actual
colours. When He bids us be perfect even as His
heavenly Father is perfect, He is looking within at
His own inner world and contemplating His own
intimate union with God. And entering thus into
Himself and realizing the marvellous actuality of

[1] *Mt.* xxii, 37-39.   [2] *Mt.* vii, 16, *sqq.*
[3] *Mk.* x, 27.

that union, He turns to all those who wish to be His disciples and demands the like of them. So that His demands, which to the natural man seem extravagant, are seen to be not so much demands as promises and luminous ideals for all those who receive Him, who believe in Him, who become one flesh and one blood with Him.

Therefore His austere moral commandments are to be regarded as implying His Messianic love and as presupposing His intention to share with all who believe in Him the riches of His union with God and the power that comes from that union. They fall from the lips of our Redeemer and have the cadence of His redeeming love. They are intended not for the unbeliever, but for the believer, and their purpose is to define more clearly the path and goal of our life with Jesus in the Christian fellowship. They presuppose His redemptive will and His intention of bestowing by grace on all those who believe in Him, His own spirit and His own strength.

How does Jesus display this redemptive will and purpose of bestowing grace? He displays it over and over again in the Gospels, and especially— where we should least expect it—in His encounters with the possessed. At first the demoniac shuns

Him; his sin-distorted being feels the presence of something foreign and hostile to itself, the manifestation of holiness. And that holiness so works upon him as to produce sudden fright and wild terror. But, His presence continuing, the demoniac yields more and more to the influence of His grace. He is like a child who first struggles wildly against the ministrations of the physician, and then goes to sleep in his ministering arms. The power of Jesus, awakening and sanctifying, penetrates deeper and deeper into the poor soul; and at last a new thing is formed in him, a new will and a new strength, and he becomes whole in body and soul. 'And when he went up into the ship, he that had been troubled with the devil began to beseech him that he might be with him.' [1] So great was the power of love that went forth from Jesus, that the demoniac who before had dwelt in tombs and was so crazy that 'no man could bind him, not even with chains,' [2] now wished no more to leave Him. He was bound with new bonds, the bonds of the love of Jesus.

We may take it for certain fact that Jesus undertook no healing of the body which was not at the same time a healing of the soul. The evangelists

[1] *Mk.* v, 18.   [2] *Mk.* v, 3.

for their apologetic purposes emphasize those
bodily cures which, falling visibly under men's
eyes, made Jews and pagans realize the saving
power of our Lord. But His thought and purpose
were so entirely subordinated to the glory of His
Father and the establishment of His Kingdom, and
He Himself was so completely and absolutely
identified with holiness, that we cannot think of
His action except as a comprehensive effort
embracing both body and soul. At Capharnaum
they brought to Him a man sick of the palsy, and
not being able to get to Him for the crowd, they
let down the sick man through an opening in the
roof.[1] In his narrative of that healing St. Mark
indicates quite plainly that Jesus saw sickness and
sin, the affections of body and soul, in one com-
bined whole, and healed them together. The
paralytic looks to our Lord with anxious, appealing eyes, expecting from Him a bodily healing.
But Jesus does not immediately say, 'Take up thy
bed and go into thy house'; He speaks first of
something apparently quite remote from the situa-
tion and wholly unexpected by the sick man: 'Son,
thy sins are forgiven thee.' What He sees first
and before all else is not the paralyzed body but

[1] *Mk.* ii, 3 *sqq.*

121

the tormented soul. And it is only after the soul
is healed that He goes on to confound the Scribes
who in their hearts were censuring Him for
claiming to forgive sins and to free the paralytic
from his bodily sickness. 'But that you may know
that the Son of Man hath power on earth to forgive sins, I say to thee, Arise, take up thy bed,
and go into thy house.' We may certainly take
this case as a standard example of our Lord's
miracles of healing, and it shows clearly that He
healed soul as well as body. The whole man,
body and soul alike, appertains to Jesus and is
subject to His redemptive power.

No one came to Jesus, with hunger and thirst
of soul, but found refreshment in that spiritual
strength and moral purity which flowed from Him
as a stream of living water, as He Himself expresses it.[1] So strong at first was the impression of
His purity and holiness that the sinner seemed
hardly able to bear His presence. 'Depart from
me, O Lord, for I am a sinful man,' cried St.
Peter,[2] feeling keenly that he could not face such
purity, and that whatever light was in him would
in this radiance be utterly extinguished. The cen-
turion of Capharnaum with his 'Lord, I am not

[1] *Jn.* vii, 38.   [2] *Lk.* v, 8.

worthy that thou shouldst enter under my roof'
expressed a profound and genuine sense of his
insufficiency in face of the purity of our Lord.[1]

But this negative effect was succeeded at once
by a positive one. In that nocturnal conference
of His with Nicodemus, Jesus Himself described
this positive and novel effect as a re-birth in the
Holy Spirit. 'Unless a man be born again, he
cannot see the kingdom of God.'[2] And with a
master's hand He portrayed the working-out of
this new power in that inimitable figure of the
vine and its branches. 'I am the vine, you the
branches. He that abideth in me and I in him,
the same beareth much fruit, for without me you
can do nothing.'[3] In the synoptic gospels also
this new life is described as living with Jesus and
drawing strength from His abundance. 'Come to
me all you that labour and are burdened and I
will refresh you. Take up my yoke upon you and
learn of me, because I am meek and humble of
heart. And you shall find rest for your souls.'[4]

The most striking example of our Lord's work
in the healing of the soul is furnished for us by
St. Luke in his account of the sinner who anointed

[1] *Mt.* viii, 8.
[2] *Jn.* iii, 3.
[3] *Jn.* xv, 5.
[4] *Mt.* xi, 28, 29.

our Lord's feet.[1] St. Luke indeed mentions her
conversion only in passing, for he is telling us
rather of the Pharisee's hostility than of her love.
But that only makes the simple story of her
conversion all the more effective. 'And standing
behind at his feet she began to wash his feet with
tears, and wiped them with the hairs of her head,
and kissed his feet and anointed them with the
ointment.' In this description of her conduct, St.
Luke reveals to us the whole history of her soul.
When she saw Jesus first and first heard Him
speak, He had stirred her soul to its depths. Scales
seemed to fall from her eyes. She was standing
in sin, and around her was dark night. But yon-
der was one standing in light, who was Himself
wholly light. Could she get to that light? Was
there a way to Him? There was a way, but it
was barred by many a familiar figure. There they
were, crowned with the roses of pleasure and
holding the brimming cups of delight; and her
soul was attached to them. She had turned away
from God and bestowed herself on the merely
human. She was sunk in the wretchedness of our
fallen nature. Yet she heard as from afar the
alluring words, summoning her to cross to the

[1] *Lk.* vii, 37 *sqq.*

light: 'Blessed are the pure of heart, for they shall see God.' Should she walk into the land of purity? In her breast was the wild cry: 'Thou canst not, thou mayest not!' Her whole being had drunk deep of sin, and she fought desperately against the light that came from Jesus. But that light seemed to shine ever purer and brighter. A new heart was already being formed within her. And finally, she entered Simon's house; let folk say what they might and let Simon judge her never so cruelly. She clasped the feet of the Lord and uttered her confession with tears of repentance. And the Good Shepherd turned to her and said: 'Thy sins are forgiven thee.' What bird had ever made such sweet music in her ears? What breeze of spring had ever blown so gently and so softly over the hills? Stronger and more powerful, for all their quiet simplicity, than any decree of the Emperor in Rome, were these words of the Lord: 'Thy sins are forgiven thee.'

That is Jesus and His redeeming power, as we see it in the gospels in an endless variety of forms. Let us now ask where lie the roots of this power, and what is its deepest source. With this question we push forward to the ultimate cause which makes Jesus our Redeemer and makes us Christians His redeemed.

From what we have heard already about Jesus the perfect teacher and Jesus the wonder-worker the answer to our question must have already forced itself upon our attention. We must have realized that the ultimate source and deepest cause of His blessed activity could only be His divinity. Only because Jesus is no ordinary man, only because He is at the same time God, only because He is the revelation of absolute truth, purity and holiness, is He full of grace and truth for mankind.

And having given this answer we have proclaimed an infinitely sublime truth. For so it is, if Jesus were not God, He could not be our Redeemer. For the redemption of mankind involved our deliverance from a twofold servitude. We had to be delivered from the bonds of merely natural being, so fragmentary and limited and transient, so utterly inadequate and unsatisfactory; and we had to be delivered from attachment to sin, with all its fatal effects upon soul and body, with remorse and death in its train. Granted a living God, it rests with Him alone whether we shall be raised from the remote and desolate abyss of our natural being, and out of the still remoter wretchedness of our sin, to the infinite riches of His personal life. On our side there is no means of coming to the divine life. Our imperfect being nowhere marches with the divine being. There is between us and God an abyss which can be bridged by God's act alone. All human action, even at its best, so far as it is purely human, is impaired by the limitations of the creature, and corroded by imperfection and sin. In the light of God's infinite majesty and holiness any merely human excellence is infinitesimally small and scarcely to be perceived. In that light there is no great distance between John the beloved disciple and Judas the traitor, for in comparison with the divine perfection their own natural value is as nothing. Even the human will of Jesus, for all its purity, could not bear comparison with the infinite holiness of the divine will, and He refused to be called good: 'Why callest thou me good? None is good but God alone.' [1] Therefore to speak of 'self-redemption' is vain madness; for none but God can redeem us. It was this conviction that gave the struggle against the Arians for the true divinity of our Lord, its ardour and its dogged determination, the conviction that if our Redeemer were not true God then we were still in our sins.

[1] *Mk.* x, 18.

It is only because He is the Son of God that His redemptive work has an infinite merit, a value in God's sight, a superabundant saving value. Only a divine Redeemer can bridge the infinite chasm which separates man from God.

But this truth, that our Redeemer is very God, is not the whole truth. Were His divine nature everything, our faith would be something like the faith of early Christian Gnosticism. Christ Himself would not be true man, and would stand for nothing more than that sublime moment in history in which mankind enjoyed an immediate experience of the justice and mercy of God, and in which the just and gracious God acted directly upon us. Were that the case we could indeed trust ourselves to this divine revelation and we should have a road provided for our journey to God. But we should have had to travel this way very much by ourselves, in the exercise of our free will and its free moral choice. It would have depended on our own single-handed co-operation with divine grace whether we should ever get to God. We should have had no mediator and no mediatorial merits to help us, and we should have found it hard to keep a firm footing. On the one side would have been the just God, offering us His grace, inviting us and helping us in His love; and on the other we should have stood alone. And if, according to the old Protestant view of justification, the effect of original sin was to wreck our human nature and deprive us of all power of moral and religious action, then we should have had in ourselves no firm support whatever for the struggle of life, but should have been subject wholly to the incalculable decree and arbitrary decision of God. Like some meteorite hurled into empty space, man would have fallen into the abyss of his creaturely limitations and his sins, and would have had no hope save in the blind trust of faith that God would somehow wonderfully lay hold on him and bring him home.

The plain defect of this Protestant theory of redemption is that it exaggerates the impotence of fallen man to an intolerable degree. It seems to exhibit the same decadent mood that we found before in the Judaism of the Hellenistic period. But a profounder defect of the theory is this, that it fails to appreciate the importance of the humanity of Jesus in the work of our redemption. It sees in Him only the just and gracious God; it does not see the human Mediator and High Priest, the meritorious cause of our salvation. And modern Protestantism shows the same defect. According to the teaching of a prominent Lutheran theologian (Karl Heim) the humanity of Jesus has only a symbolical value, as the means through which we experience the mercy of God. Jesus is not a Mediator, at once God and Man, who truly and really takes our sins upon Himself and wins forgiveness for us. So also in the modern Calvinism of Karl Barth the humanity of Christ is equally unimportant. Like every other human creature it is subject to the law of death, and death is its end; but Christ uses its death to teach His lesson of eternal life. That is the whole of its function. And in America there are wide areas where Protestantism has lost all faith in a Redeemer, giving our Lord the status only of a moral example.

But all is not well even among Catholics. For there is among us a good deal of pious feeling and devout prayer which would seem to ignore the humanity of Jesus and His mediatorship, as though there were but two things—God and the soul— and as though the whole responsibility for our redemption lay upon us men alone. In our Lord we regard only the divine element, the Word of God, and we do not consider, or at least not deeply enough, His humanity and mediatorship. It is true that we use and intend those glad words

'Through Christ our Lord,' but we do not realize and experience their full meaning. We act as though all depended on our own good will, and as though we could ourselves reach out after God's grace and attain beatitude. And so it happens inevitably that the devout soul in its solitary struggle for grace becomes perplexed and troubled. The God of grace becomes a God of wrath; the primitive Jewish spirit of fear and servility drives out the liberty and happiness of the child of God; and finally the soul is captured by scrupulosity and religious mania.

We have in that a very plain illustration of the necessary connection between dogma and life. The Christian does not realize the full meaning of redemption, because he does not grasp the mystery of Christ in its totality. For the full Christ is not God alone; He is God and Man, He is God Incarnate.

Why is the Incarnation of God the decisive thing? Because we now have among us a Man who is God. We have a Brother who is God. Our own flesh and blood, our human nature, is no longer cursed of God, but blessed. It is raised from out of its negation and nothingness to positive fulness. We are made members of the family

131

of God. The Incarnation has bridged the gulf which divided us from God, and our human nature is now in Christ united with God. For in Him it entered into the most intimate union imaginable with the divinity, a union so complete and true that the divine and human natures have but one personality between them, the Second Person of the Blessed Trinity, the Word of God.

But how does this miracle of the Incarnation, worked thus in one human nature, benefit the whole of mankind? It does so because it was the divine Word that became man. Precisely because it was the creative principle itself that took human nature, Christ as the God-Man has become the creative principle of a new humanity. He is not merely a man, He is *the* Man; not one individual member of mankind, but the Head of mankind, its new beginning, the first-born among His brethren, the new Adam. Just as the first Adam, the progenitor of the human race, according to the special design of God, was not a man like us other men, but was *the* man, the God-appointed representative of the whole race who in himself contained germinally all possible men, the personification of mankind, the one single man whose fall and fate were to be the fall and fate of all men, so our Lord, by virtue of His union with the Godhead, is the origin and starting point of a new race of men. He is the new Man in whom all other men called to salvation are potentially present, and whose life and fate are our life and fate also. As regards their relation to mankind, Adam and Christ are distinct only in this, that the connection of men with the first Adam depends upon the natural unity of the race and is therefore spontaneously effected in corporeal generation, whereas our solidarity with Christ is based upon a spiritual, or rather supernatural, act—upon the divine self-giving—and is therefore shared by us only through a spiritual act, the act of self-surrender. But in both cases the same truth holds: both Adam and Christ represent and connote all men that are called to salvation. And the Second Adam, God Incarnate, stands in a necessary relation to all redemption-needing mankind. In Himself and by Himself He is not as yet the complete Christ, for He becomes so only when all the redeemed have been incorporated into Him. They are His fulness.[1] He is the Head and they are the members; He is the vine and they are the branches. When we speak of Christ we imply the whole Christian fellowship, for there can be no isolated

[1] *Eph.* iv, 13.

and solitary Christ. There is only the full and complete Christ, wherein Head and members form one Body.

And therefore also there can be no isolated and solitary Christian, for with every Christian there is Christ and the fulness of His members. Consequently we do not face God in isolation and loneliness; we come before Him in Christ, united in a profound union with His only-begotten Son. Just as breathing and feeling and thinking are functions of our natural being, so living in Christ is a function of our Christian being. Christ is the new sphere in which our whole religious life is to be lived: our prayer and penance, our thanksgiving and joy. And even our natural activities, which must at bottom be controlled by religion, are exercised within this sphere: our daily work, our achievements, our struggles, our suffering and our dying. The Christian never toils and suffers and dies *alone,* that word is absent from his vocabulary. Christianity is a living and dying in full fellowship with Christ and His members.

Because we are thus, through Christ our Brother, drawn out of our isolation and raised to newness of life in Him, therefore all that Christ, the first-born of His brethren, has done for us, from birth

134

to death, belongs truly and really to us. All is ours: His teaching, His miracles, His hunger and thirst and sorrow and passion and death. The whole vast work which the Incarnate Word achieved from Bethlehem to Calvary—that marvellous work of single-hearted devotion to the will of His Father, before whom the angels veil their faces and sanctity itself grows dim—belongs in the fullest sense to us Christians. 'The Passion of Christ,' says St. Thomas Aquinas, 'belongs to us as really as though we ourselves had suffered it.' [1] Our redemption, therefore, does not mean just this, that we live our lives in the Spirit of Jesus and imitate His wondrous works. Nor does it mean that we take the merits of Christ and build up our supernatural life on that basis by our own effort. For the merits of Christ are not merely the necessary presupposition of the Christian life; they are its essential substance and the solid core of our new value in God's sight as redeemed souls. Nor is our redemption a thing which we have still to effect by our own grace-helped activity; we are already redeemed in Christ our Brother. With Him we mounted the Cross, with Him we rose again, in Him we were redeemed. The essential

[1] *Summa Theol.* iii, q. 69, a, 2.

and decisive part of all that we have to perform in order to expiate our guilt has been already performed by Him, by our Brother who is God. 'He is the propitiation for our sins; and not for ours only, but also for those of the whole world.' [1] He is in a true and genuine sense the 'Lamb of God who taketh away the sins of the world.' He has already, really and truly, paid the ransom for us. So we have, over against the justice of God, a strong support which can never fail us, the redemptive act of Christ.

This is our good tidings of great joy, that the debt of our guilt is cancelled. The sting of hopelessness has been extracted from all sin. Our duty of expiation has been in substance performed, and according to the full severity of justice abundant and superabundant satisfaction has been made. No dark barrier lies any longer between us and God; the road is open and we may go direct to Him. That is the new liberty of the Christian, for man's guilt and burden have been cleared away. God is again and finally ours, and we are God's. We are redeemed.

Since our redemption is of this nature, we can see at once why our faith teaches that the begin-

[1] *I. Jn.* ii, 2.

ning of our salvation and our perseverance in good depend upon unmerited and unmeritable grace. For us Christians there is indeed no true merit apart from our union with Christ. And, further, whenever our life of grace begins or is renewed, whenever it is greatly deepened or developed, the work is due, not to our personal moral activity and energy, but to the unmerited graces conveyed to us through one of the seven sacraments.

In the reception of these sacraments—so the Church teaches—all that we have to do is 'to put no obstacle' to grace: *nullam obicem ponere.* The expression is very significant. The Church deliberately abstains from speaking of any positive activity on our part, because she wishes under all circumstances to secure the great truth that we do not redeem ourselves, but that our redemption is the act of Christ.

If we try to express the Church's meaning positively and to define more precisely the exact manner of our co-operation with Christ in our redemption, then it is certain in the first place that our co-operation is not exhaustively described when we speak of a certain blind confidence in the grace of Christ, or 'fiducial' faith as the Protestant would call it. Of course, trust in Christ is necessary, and it is a beginning of love. But trust by itself is not enough, for trust is only one function of the soul, whereas the whole man must be given to Christ: not only feeling, but also thought, and above all heart and will. Only that man is redeemed who with faith and love affirms the redemptive act of Christ. It is true that original sin has weakened and impaired the faculties of our soul, but it has not destroyed them. Every living man is able to discern and to esteem holiness as holiness, even though he does not make it his own. Therefore every man has the capacity, and having the capacity has the duty, to accept the redemptive act of Christ with all his mind and with all his heart. My faith is genuine and true only when it grips my whole being, when I do not merely trust in Christ, but, so far as lies in me, put my thought and will, my whole ethico-religious energy, at the service of His redemption. For I must co-operate with Christ, and His work must in a measure be my work also. To put the matter in precise form, we may say that it is this action of mine which appropriates to my person the objective value of Christ's redemption and makes it a subjective reality.

In this way I make a personal contribution to the work of my redemption. But it would be a mistake to compare my personal contribution with Christ's redemption, and to regard it as though it were an independent and co-ordinate factor in that redemption. For the great benefit won for us in the Church's conflict with the semi-Pelagians was the firm establishment of the dogma that throughout the whole process of our salvation, its beginning, progress and consummation, the initiative lies exclusively with God and with His grace through Christ our Lord. Never and in no part of that process does the initiative lie with man. The co-operation of man by his faith, contrition, penance, moral effort and practical love, is never his own affair alone, or even especially his own affair; it is in the first and principal sense God's affair. That co-operation is effected 'through Christ our Lord.' Therefore in the first instance it depends not on me but on God's initiative, whether and when and how I co-operate in the process of my redemption. My personal, human action has its deepest and ultimate impulse, not in human willing, but in the loving will of the divine Redeemer.

True, the impulse of God will ever be of such a nature as to do no violence to the human will, so that man is his own master throughout. Nevertheless it remains the fact, for it is revealed truth, that man's whole contribution to his redemption is rooted in the special impulse of God's love. His human activity in a mysterious way that is hidden from us is interwoven with the divine activity. The impulse which sets us moving on the way of redemption, and decisively keeps us in motion, is nothing but God and the grace of Christ.

And therefore, regarding it fundamentally, I cannot call my co-operation my own work; it is the working of Christ in me. 'We ourselves are not life: we share the life of Christ.' [1] I cannot even 'say the Lord Jesus but by the Holy Ghost.' [2] All the vital virtue of a redeemed soul, all its truth, fidelity, purity and love, all is born of the love of our Saviour and imbued with His redeeming blood. The soul could not maintain itself for a moment in this state of virtue, were it not for His grace. So Christian morality is essentially different from a purely human morality. It implies the marvellous fact that Christ lives in the Christian man.

And therefore it depends wholly and entirely on the free choice of God, and not on men, what form this marvellous life shall take in me and to what point it shall be developed. It is God's to decide how far 'the life of Jesus shall be made manifest in

[1] St. Augustine.   [2] *I. Cor.* xii, 3.

our bodies.'[1] It depends on His grace alone whether I shall rank among the great in the kingdom of God or among the very small, whether I shall come to the Saviour's Heart without let or hindrance, or shall have to pass through sin and penance. And all the effort that I devote to the work of my salvation, all my study and all my prayer, is in its ultimate and deepest nature—where first it comes to the threshold of consciousness to pass over into the will—already the gift and grace of God, the operation of His redeeming love. In its ultimate and deepest nature it is not my own work, but the breathing of His Spirit, a profound and incalculable mystery. 'The Spirit breatheth where he will; and thou hearest his voice; but thou knowest not whence he cometh and whither he goeth. So is everyone that is born of the Spirit.'[2]

Starting then from this point, and seeking once more to determine precisely what is man's contribution in the sphere of his natural being and by his natural powers alone to the work of his redemption—what belongs to him alone and not at the same time and chiefly to the divine causality—we can only say that it is man's business to hold him-

[1] *II. Cor.* iv, 10.   [2] *Jn.* iii, 8.

141

self ready for Christ and His grace. He must be abidingly accessible and awake to Christ and His grace. To co-operate with grace means therefore nothing else than reverently to accept and bravely foster the impulse and motion which my activity has already received from God; or, more precisely, not to interrupt it perversely or wantonly arrest its course. Therefore to co-operate with grace means really to be of good will. And that was the angel's message on Christmas night: 'Peace on earth to men of good will.' Consequently my personal contribution is a very small and simple thing. In its nature it is no greater an achievement than the achievement of the little child which allows its father to lift it up that it may pluck an apple from the tree, and allows him then to take its tiny hand in his and wrench the apple loose. 'You plucked it and it is yours,' says the father to his child, and the child accepts its father's love without any resistance. And that is all that we need, the small and simple acceptance of the little child.

And so we get a clear understanding of the meaning and substance of our Christianity. To be a Christian means to be redeemed, not through one's own strength, but 'through Christ our Lord.' To be a Christian means the knowledge that I have

all in Christ. Where Christ is, there is no anxiety
or fear. No part of His teaching is plainer than
His insistence on cheerful courage. 'Be of good
heart, son.' 'Be of good heart, daughter.' And He
condemns nothing so decisively as worry and fear.
'Why are you fearful, O ye of little faith?' [1]
'Peace be with you. It is I, fear not.' [2] That teaching is valid not only for the natural life, but for
the supernatural life also, with its difficulties and
dangers. It is especially applicable to anxiety
regarding sin. Where Christ is, this anxiety is
banished. For the new life does not consist chiefly
in an anxious struggle with sin, but in gallant love
for Christ. That is why St. Francis of Sales warns
us to have more love for good than fear of evil.
It is possible that we may fall into sin again and
again. Where is the Christian who has not fallen?
It is not immunity from sin that makes a Christian; but the Christian is one who when he falls
gets up quickly, who calls at once upon Jesus from
the depths of his sin, who allows himself to be
raised again and again by His hand. Wherever
there is such a loving faith and faithful love, such
an unlimited confidence in Christ, the soul is sure
of attaining the Father, though it seem often to

[1] *Mt.* viii, 26.   [2] *Lk.* xxiv, 36.

stray from the path, by dangerous abyss and treacherous swamp, and though it be sometimes tossed on the wild billows of a stormy sea, so that it is forced to cry, 'Lord, save me, I perish.'

Therefore the gospel of Jesus is in a true and deep and glad sense an *evangelium,* good tidings, telling of the new freedom of the redeemed. 'Rejoice in the Lord always; again I say, rejoice.' [1] Christianity is joy in the Lord. Christianity is the faith that moves mountains. Christianity is constant thanksgiving. 'Giving thanks always for all things, in the name of our Lord Jesus Christ, to God and the Father.' [2] For verily and indeed we are redeemed. *Deo gratias!*

[1] *Phil.* iv, 4.   [2] *Eph.* v, 20.

CHAPTER VI

COME, HOLY GHOST!

AT Whitsuntide nature keeps high festival.
Around us we see an overflowing energy of life, in
flower and shrub and tree, in bird and in beast.
It is an abundant, even an extravagant life. The
power that called such luxuriance into being was
no niggardly power, no miser dealing out his
favours with anxious calculation. Consider the
millions of blossoms, spread lavishly in field and
wood, of which but a small fraction will ever come
to fruit or seed. What generous luxuriance, splen-
did extravagance, rich exuberance! And out of
this unstinted largesse spring the beauty of the
world, its gay abundance, its rich and varied play
of form and scent and colour.

There seems a special appropriateness in such
splendour at Whitsuntide, when we are celebrating
the feast of the Holy Spirit. It seems emblematic
of His power, the rich language of abundant
natural life announcing the great Giver of spiritual

life. For it is the proper and characteristic quality of the Holy Spirit that He is the creative Spirit, the giver of the new life and of the abundant fulness of that life. That is the Church's meaning when she addresses the Holy Spirit, in the vesper hymn, as 'Creative Spirit' (*Creator Spiritus*), when she hails Him as 'fountain of life' (*fons vivus*) and as 'fire' (*ignis*); and when in the liturgy of the Mass she prays: 'Send forth Thy Spirit and they shall be created; and Thou shalt renew the face of the earth.'

This creative, vivifying, enkindling quality of the Holy Spirit is His special attribute. It is true that in theological usage the title of Creator is particularly appropriated to God the Father, and again, that St. John seems to attach it to the Son, for 'all things were made by him, and without him was made nothing that was made.' [1] The fact is, of course, that in all God's activity *ad extra,* that is, beyond the sphere of His own divine life, the three divine Persons work together in an inseparable union. They share one and the selfsame divine Nature; and they are so interlocked in reciprocal compenetration and comprehension that they may indeed be distinguished, but cannot be

[1] *Jn.* i, 3.

146

separated, not even in thought. Consequently, as the one Triune God, the three Persons work together to one and the same effect, whether that be creation, redemption or sanctification. But, on the other hand, because they possess one identical divine Nature in various manners—the Father in one way, as the source and origin of the whole Godhead; the Son in another, as eternally begotten by the Father; and the Holy Ghost in yet another, as proceeding from Father and Son—therefore their extra-divine activity, though the activity of one and the same divine Nature, can be distinguished according to the manner in which each single Person possesses that divine Nature. Therefore the relations of the three divine Persons to one another within the Trinity have their counterpart in the activity of those three Persons outside the life of the Trinity. Hence the justification of that 'appropriation' whereby theology assigns certain special functions to one or other of the three Persons, according to the special characteristics of that Person. So, following the guidance of revelation, theology assigns creation to the Father and redemption to the Son, not implying that these acts belong exclusively to those Persons, but asserting that the special qualities of Father and Son re-

CHRIST OUR BROTHER

spectively are manifested in these acts and justify
that particular appropriation.

It is not therefore inappropriate, nor is it any
mere manner of speaking, when we address the
Holy Spirit in particular as the superabundant,
creative source of all extra-divine activity. For it
is the special property of the Holy Spirit to be the
outpouring of the life and love of God. He is
that gracious, holy, mighty love, resultant of the
eternal love of Father and Son, wherein those two
divine Persons, surrendering their exclusive per-
sonalities, give themselves one to the other in an
infinite fulness of love. And if the Son is that
divine Other, whom the Father in mysterious
process of eternal substantial self-comprehension
begets from all eternity as His image and co-eternal
reflection, so is the Holy Spirit that divine Union,
wherein Father and Son meet in an unending commerce of superabundant life. He is the 'embrace
of Father and Son,' the 'Kiss of Father and Son,' [1]
the 'outpouring of the divine life.' [2] And since
the life of God is essentially love and sanctity, He
is the 'flower and fragrance of the sanctity of
Father and Son, just as He is the culmination of
their spirituality.' [2] But when we try to grasp His

[1] *St. Bernard.*　　　　　[2] *Scheeben.*

148

procession from Father and Son thought fails us and language is all inadequate. We can only attempt to describe it as an outpouring and over-flowing of love and holiness that flows from Father and Son, and shining forth in its own independent selfhood is always the perfection of self-giving and fulness of intercommunion.

From out of this fulness came creation. It is true that the act of creation is appropriated to the Father, inasmuch as creation more than any other of the works of God reflects the Father's special property of being the source of all reality, the Blessed Trinity itself included. But as creation does not proceed from any inner necessity of God, but rather is an act of His free and generous love, in that respect it is the work of the Holy Spirit. If God were only pure intelligence and could express Himself only in His Word, then there could be no world distinct from God. For even the most perfect of all possible worlds, being created out of nothingness, would fall infinitely short of the perfection of God and would be no proper object for His creative activity. All philosophical systems which have regarded God exclusively as absolute intelligence, as pure thought, have been forced to deny any essential distinction between God and the world, and so either to deify the world or to bring God down to its level. They have all ended in some form or other of pantheism. Nor can we regard creation as the effect of divine will alone. For a blind, unreasoning will would only grope in darkness and form an irrational world. Then a most arid pessimism would be the final end of philosophy. Rather it is because God is not merely thought and will but also goodness, and because He communicates His goodness in the most generous love, that the creation of the world is possible. In the Blessed Trinity the goodness of God is not merely a divine attribute, but is also perfectly realized in an autonomous Person, with the consequence that there is a possibility of action beyond the sphere of the Godhead, and a motive for the creation of the world. A love that is so fruitful that it blazes forth from all eternity out of the divine fulness of life into a special Person flows for its own sake beyond the divine sphere in order to give itself to creatures. Therefore creation is not merely the work of the Father, who as the ground of all existence calls the world forth from nothingness; nor is it merely the work of the Son, whose image it bears; it is also an act of the Holy Ghost, because it is a work of creative and abounding love. Hence the pregnant words of *Genesis:* 'And the Spirit of God moved over the waters.' [1] Hence those words of *Wisdom* with which the Whitsunday Mass begins: 'The Spirit of the Lord hath filled the whole world.' [2] And the psalms of the Office for Whitsuntide celebrate with joyful rapture the creative might of God:

> 'O Lord, my God, thou art exceeding great!
> Thou hast put on praise and beauty:
> And art clothed with light as with a garment.
> Who stretches out the heaven like a pavilion:
> Who coverest the higher rooms thereof with water.
> Who makest the clouds thy chariot:
> Who walkest upon the wings of the winds.' [3]

Wherever we turn in the luxuriant springtide, whether to the radiant flowers of the wayside, or to the glad song of the birds, or to the bright laughter of human children, everywhere and in all things there greets us the Holy Spirit and His abounding love.

But that evidence of the Spirit is more intimate still—the most intimate thing we have on earth—which meets us in the region of the supernatural. Who has ever grasped the riches of God's prodigal generosity and the depths of His self-communicating love which the supernatural life of our souls

---

[1] *Gen.* i, 2. [2] *Wisdom* i, 7. [3] *Ps.* ciii, 1-3.

implies? That life means redemption from Satan, from sin and from death, through Him who gave Himself a redemption for many. There is now no more any ban, or curse, or interdict. Nor is that all. Redemption might have entailed no more than this, that man should be restored to the state whence he had fallen, that is, to pure nature and to that nature's destiny. We should then have been free again to love and serve God with our nature's natural powers. We should have been able to give ourselves to God in such service; yet there would have been no giving of God Himself to us. But the supernatural life implies this latter gift, for in it we become sharers in the divine nature. Beyond all claims and powers of our finite being, we are so far made divine that we become members of His race and His children who can cry to Him: Abba, Father! That is love without limit, that is abounding generosity, that is the Holy Spirit. True it is that our nature was raised to this height by the work of the Son; for He is our Saviour, who gave us of the life which He had had from all eternity with His Father. But this work of our salvation was made possible and made possible in its infinite generosity—so that the infinite Word entered into finite time and took the form of man, yes, of

sinful man, and then incarnate gave up all, even
His life itself, for His brethren—by the Holy Spirit.
He, the personal loving union of Father and Son,
is the true source and fount whence comes the su-
perabundance of God's love towards men. 'The
divine nature is communicated from Father to Son
by eternal generation, and then from both in eternal love to the Holy Spirit. It is only in this second
communication that God can come to man. And
so the Holy Spirit, who is the resultant of the unity
of Father and Son, appears also as the mediator of
that unity between God and the creature which is
formed on the model of the former.' [1] The
redemptive work of Jesus and the new supernatural life which it has brought to us, are most
profoundly and intimately grounded in that mystery of Personal Love which is the Holy Spirit.
And therefore 'no man can say the Lord Jesus but
by the Holy Ghost.' [2] The evangelists indicate
skilfully those particular moments in the life of
Jesus in which the loving outpouring of the Holy
Spirit is especially plain: His Incarnation; [3] His
consecration as Messiah; [4] His fasting in the desert,
temptation and victory; [5] His casting out of devils

[1] *Scheeben.*　　[2] *I. Cor.* xii, 3.　　[3] *Lk.* i, 35; *Mt.* i, 20.
[4] *Lk.* iii, 21.　　[5] *Lk.* iv, 1.

from the possessed [1]—all of which attest the working of the Holy Spirit. And does He not Himself in like manner explain the mystery of His humanity in those words of Isaias: 'The Spirit of the Lord is upon me, wherefore he hath anointed me.' [2] The human life of Jesus is bright with the radiance of the Holy Spirit. In every work of His we can descry the influence of the spirit of love.

And yet the abounding love of the Holy Spirit is not revealed to its full in the life of our Lord. For it is one of the deepest mysteries of God's divine counsel, that though our redemption was completely achieved by Jesus, yet each of us can only attain it by the Holy Spirit. Jesus, the perfect Man, perfectly obedient to God, offered His sinless body in voluntary loving sacrifice for His brethren, and by that sacrifice destroyed once and for all the document of guilt which separated us from God. In the sacrificial vesture of our humanity He established and secured the objective basis of our salvation. But, at the same time, He connected its subjective realization, the actual attaining by each individual of the new life, with the interposition of a new, supernatural reality, that is, with the outpouring of the Holy Spirit. 'I send the

[1] *Mt.* xii, 28.　　　　[2] *Lk.* iv, 18; *Is.* lxi, 1.

promise of my Father upon you; but stay you in the city until you be endued with power from on high.' [1] 'I will ask the Father and He shall give you another Advocate, that he may abide with you for ever.' [2] Therefore Jesus did not of Himself provide the consummation. He inaugurated the new life and laid open the way to it; but He did not perfect it. Its completion and perfection come with the comforter, the Holy Spirit. That Spirit is not a spirit foreign to Jesus, and still less is He hostile to Jesus. He is the Spirit of Jesus. 'He shall receive of mine and show it to you.' [3] The Holy Spirit will carry on the work of Jesus and establish it in the world.

We see more plainly here than anywhere else how the whole work of our redemption is pervaded by the united action of the three Persons in one God. The one God necessarily exists not as Father and Son alone, but as Father, Son and Holy Spirit, and the Holy Spirit, closing in His substantial love the infinite circle of the divinity, completes and perfects the divine life. In the same way the divine work of redemption does not belong to Father and Son alone, but to Father, Son and Holy Spirit, and it is the Holy Spirit that completes and

[1] *Lk.* xxiv, 49.   [2] *Jn.* xiv, 16.   [3] *Jn.* xvi, 14.

perfect it. In His action our redemption and
Christian life culminate in such sort that without
the Holy Ghost and His fulfilling there would be
no complete Christianity. So distinctive and
important is this fulfilling by the Spirit that the
prophets of the Old Covenant recognized it as a
characteristic of the Messianic age, and prophesied
its coming. 'And it shall come to pass after this
that I will pour out my spirit upon all flesh; and
your sons and your daughters shall prophesy. . . .
Moreover, upon my servants and handmaids in
those days I will pour forth my spirit.'[1] The
early Christians obviously believed that the
Messianic Age had brought with it the fulness of
the Spirit. In his speech on the day of Pentecost,
St. Peter expressly appealed to the prophecy of
Joel.[2] And they regarded themselves as inspired
by the Spirit,[3] as living under the law of the
Spirit,[4] as signed with the sign of the Spirit.[5]
St. Paul regards the Spirit as the distinguishing
mark of a Christian.[6] According to St. John,[7]

[1] *Joel* ii, 28, *sqq.; cf.
Ezech.* xxxvi, 26, *sqq.; Is.*
xliv, 3, *sqq.*

[2] *Acts* ii. 16.

[3] *Gal.* vi, 1; *I. Cor.* ii,
15; iii, 1.

[4] *Rom.* viii, 2.

[5] *Eph.* i, 14.

[6] *Gal.* iii, 1, *sqq.; II. Cor.*
xi, 4.

[7] *I. Jn.* iv, 13.

156

we know that 'we abide in him and he in us' by the fact that 'he hath given us of his spirit.' So profoundly is this fulness of the Spirit experienced that it overrides all merely human wisdom and all purely human authorities and regulations. 'The spiritual man judgeth all things, and he himself is judged of no man.' [1] The glad assurance of redemption comes from the Spirit: 'For the Spirit himself giveth testimony to our spirit that we are the sons of God.' [2] He is the 'pledge' which is given in our hearts. [3] The same spirit gives confident outspokenness; [4] glad readiness for sacrifice, [5] and true fellowship. [6] So exuberantly rich is this Spirit that He expresses Himself in the most various gifts, which are granted to the individual soul 'according to the measure of the giving of Christ,' [7] and which show themselves particularly in 'speaking with tongues' or ecstatic prayer, in 'prophecy' or the power of edifying discourse, and in healing. The so-called *we* passages of the Acts [8] are quite full of this enthusiastic joy in the

---

[1] *I. Cor.* ii, 15.
[2] *Rom.* viii, 16.
[3] *II. Cor.* i, 22.
[4] παρρησία, *Acts* ii, 29; iv, 13, 31; xxviii, 31.
[5] *Acts* v, 41; *II. Cor.* iv. 8, *sqq.*
[6] *Acts* iv, 32, *sqq.*
[7] *Eph.* iv, 7, *sqq.*
[8] *Acts* xvi, 10-17; xx, 5-xxi, 18; xxvii, 1-xxviii, 16.

Spirit. Prophetical figures such as Agabus, the four daughters of the apostle Philip, and the disciples of Tyre come and go in the narrative. The early Church—it is plain—feels that she has no other than the Spirit of Christ,[1] and the 'mind of Christ.'[2] At the same time the Church took care that the revelations of the Spirit should be tested by their content[3] and that no extravagances should come in,[4] yet without 'extinguishing' the Spirit.[5] 'Be zealous to prophesy; and forbid not to speak with tongues.'[6] 'And I would have you all to speak with tongues, but rather to prophesy.'[7] For in these charismata the Church recognized a decisive 'showing of the Spirit and of power.'[8] So early Christianity is marked by this enthusiastic, immediate experience of the Spirit. The Spirit was then indeed 'poured out upon all flesh.'

We can readily understand that such an abounding life of the Spirit, with the great strain which it must have put upon the faculties of the soul, could not be a permanent state of things. This outpouring of the Spirit was a concomitant of the youth of the Church. The souls of men had been

[1] I. Jn. iv, 2; I. Cor. xii, 3.
[2] I. Cor. ii, 16; ii, 2; xiv, 37.
[3] I. Thess. v, 21.
[4] I. Cor. xiv, 40.
[5] I. Thess. v, 19.
[6] I. Cor. xiv, 39.
[7] I. Cor. xiv, 5.
[8] I. Cor. ii, 4.

yearning for this revelation of the divine, and when it came through the witnesses of the Resurrection, their persons and activity, and through the great events of the day of Pentecost, it brought with it an immense and overwhelming impression of the completely new, supernatural and divine. The Spirit passed over the barren hearts of men like the warm wind of spring that awakens the hidden life of tree and flower and seed-filled ground. Add to that the widespread belief in the proximate return of Christ—in that 'little while' which was all that divided them from His coming—and we can understand the storm and stress and ecstasy of these workings of the Spirit. But, as Easter Day and Pentecost receded, as Christianity became acclimatized to the world, as Christians gradually ceased to expect a proximate Second Coming of Christ, these manifestations of the Spirit grew fainter and fainter. They had no further place in God's designs; for their purpose had been to proclaim the young faith in the face of a pagan world as the power of God, and that purpose was now achieved. And when similar manifestations afterwards make a spasmodic appearance in this or that enthusiastic group—as among the disciples of Montanus—we find that they have lost contact with the Church, and do not flow from her vigorous life. They are now manifestations of sectarianism.

Yet, however, much there may have been in the first enthusiasm of the infant Church that belonged strictly to its own time, and the circumstances of that time, its central substance, a joyful faith in the Holy Spirit, in His gifts and the life of grace which they create, was maintained in Christianity, and constitutes now, as in the beginning, its novelty and characteristic content. Christianity now as in the beginning is an outpouring of the Spirit, an experience like the experience of Pentecost; and wherever there is no such experience, there the Paraclete has not come. There are those who believe in the Father and who fancy that they are Christians because they pray to the Father for His gifts. There are those again who believe in the 'Word,' and finding in Him the meaning of all existence, strive to shape their lives according to that sublime meaning. They are men of a deep moral earnestness and of a strong sense of duty; but they are not men of the Holy Spirit, of abounding love, of glad enthusiasm. They are men for whom Pentecost has not yet come.

And how is Pentecost to come to them? In other words, how does the Holy Spirit reveal

160

Himself, even in this our day, to the sons of men? We answer that He reveals Himself not otherwise than in the first morning of creation when 'the Spirit of God moved over the waters,' and not otherwise than in the second creation, when He formed that second universe of new men, the Church of Christ. As in the beginning, in the abundance of His communicative love, He stirred the dead earth to wondrous life and beauty, and as in the mighty wind of Pentecost and its tongues of fire, He awakened and kindled souls to novel experience and strange speech, so does He work still in the Church as the creator of the 'new man,' [1] as the giver of 're-birth,' [2] or—as our Lord Himself expresses it—as a sacred 'fountain of water springing up into life everlasting.' [3]

He works through His grace. And what is that? Grace is essentially a springing up and overflowing in me of God's love; it is the breathing of the Holy Spirit in my soul, a breath of love. The power of the Holy Spirit penetrates my human soul and enters not merely into the structure of its acts of thought and will, but deeper still, to that place where my being is still the pure undifferentiated oneness of my selfhood. It penetrates to

[1] *II. Cor.* v, 17.   [2] *Jn.* iii, 5.   [3] *Jn.* iv, 14.

the centre of my soul. From out of this innermost depth, from the very roots of my being, it allures and calls, urges and draws me to God. Grace is nought else but a divine impulse which, working deep down in the human soul, gives rise to moods and yearnings which make the heart homesick for God. These moods come gradually more and more into the clear day of consciousness, and there are transformed into clear notions, desires and demands. The Holy Spirit 'stands at the door and knocks'; but He does not break the door open, for grace never overmasters free-will. It follows the way of love, it is God making love to man; and the language of love is persuasion, not force. There is nothing that works more intimately and purely and tenderly than this pressing divine love. The intellect that is gripped by it is not drawn aside from the paths of logic, but becomes a sound and healthy intellect. And it is so because, helped by the divine impulse, it acquires a deeper sensitiveness and sagacity, and a fuller appreciation of the inward side of reality—where the substance of things is touched by the finger of God—and especially of those ultimate principles upon which all reality is based and without which it becomes an empty dream. For grace gives clearness of

162

vision. Both in nature and in supernature it descries realities that remain hidden to him who deliberately represses its impulse. It has been told of a distinguished Protestant that, walking once in the Black Forest, he happened upon a simple Catholic medal dropped by some wayfarer, and that at the sight of that simple, unpretentious medal there flashed upon him, as in some magic light, the whole marvellous structure of Catholic doctrine. Nor did this vision ever leave him in peace until he had become a Catholic and a priest.

Furthermore, the grace of faith grips a man in the centre of his life and thought, and transfigures his human thinking with the warmth and glow of personal experience. It confirms the judgment of faith with all that manifold satisfaction and contentment which the soul feels when it answers the invitation of God's love. The deep conviction of faith can be the effect only of this grace. Home, school and Church all have their part in the formation of faith; but such influences are able to deal with the individual soul in a general way only. They come into contact with the personality from without, and do not penetrate to its ultimate depths, where each individual—expressing an eternally unique idea—is differentiated from every other. Only the creative Spirit, who made the individual soul, can reach that innermost shrine of personality and fashion there a faith that, growing intimately and organically out of the individual personality, determines the whole mental and moral outlook of the believer.

And there is this further point, that the new perception which comes with this grace is in some way assimilated to the divine manner of perception. 'In human faith we get no nearer to the divine nor reach its height, but merely recognize the sublimity that God's knowledge has in comparison with ours. In supernatural divine faith we are raised up even to that sublimity, in order to be made partakers of it. Through human faith we hear the voice of our Lord and Master; but through divine faith we are made friends of God and admitted into His light. . . . In the light of faith God reveals Himself immediately in the soul as Him who is speaking to it.' [1] This is that 'inward revelation,' that 'illumination of the heart,' of which the ancient theologians especially loved to speak. It rests upon external revelation and its proclamation by the Church, for it presupposes the facts of revelation. But it is

[1] Scheeben.

the perfection and culmination of the external revelation, since it issues in the highest possible personal realization of the doctrines conveyed in that revelation. That is St. John's meaning in those words of his first Epistle: 'Let the unction which you have received from him abide in you. And you have no need that any man teach you. For his unction teacheth you of all things, and is truth, and is no lie.' [1]

As a consequence, if it be genuine divine faith, the faith of a Christian is in very truth a 'showing of the spirit and of the power' of the Holy Ghost. It is not we who believe, but the Holy Ghost within us. The experience of Pentecost is continually repeated, and our faith is in its essence nothing else than the pentecostal faith of the apostles.

From out of that pentecostal faith grows the pentecostal marvel of the new man. So soon as the loving importunities of the Holy Spirit have opened the soul's eyes to God and to His truth, then that truth bursts into the confused darkness of our natural being and illumines it with its brilliant radiance. Then does a man first realize the great gulf between what he is and what he should be.

[1] *I Jn.* ii, 27.

He is afraid, trembles and draws back. But whithersoever he may go, the loving importunity of the Holy Spirit pursues him, even to the most secret recesses of his soul. The new light may pierce him, yet it is constantly giving him a new insight into things. He may kick against the goad, yet he finds himself with ever new yearnings for God and with new impulses towards good. A pitched battle begins between grace and freedom, the new love and the old, spirit and flesh, God and man; and the conflict is so fierce and thrilling, yet at the same time so glorious, that the angels of heaven rejoice to witness it.[1] That struggle has been described for us with classical lucidity by the masterly pen of St. Augustine. It is a struggle in which the fight sways this way and that. The sensual man takes refuge in unfathomable depths, in order that he may escape from the inroads of God's light—and in those depths what hell-hounds dwell and bay! When sensuality has spent its force, the devil takes a hand. The 'Prince of this World' shoots his poisoned darts into the soul of the weary combatant, and perhaps the poor soul succumbs. The unclean spirit takes possession of his house, and maybe brings with him

[1] *Lk*. xv, 10.

'seven other spirits more wicked than himself,' so that 'the last state of that man is made worse than the first.' [1]

And when this happens, to what must we ascribe the failure? Not to the divine Spirit, but to the human will. If we pursue our questioning and ask why does the human will fail, then we come face to face with a mystery. Theologians have much to say about a 'mystery of iniquity,' and speculate much regarding the inscrutable mystery of divine predestination. Yet however much the human will may be interwoven with God's saving will, a man when he sins knows very well that it is his own choice and his own decision. Man fails at the very centre his self, in that place where no demon has entry and even grace stands respectfully aloof—in the sanctuary of his being and at the heart of his personality. Such is the tragedy of the Holy Spirit of God that this deep inner man, although immersed in divine light, may yet withdraw itself from His radiance.

But when a man opens his soul to God, yes, even if he shyly and timidly make but the smallest opening for God's grace to enter, then that grace is victorious. Love comes pouring into his soul

[1] *Mt.* xii, 45.

from the heart of God, until the 'old man' grows
more and more fearful and alarmed. He is chilled
with fear and repentance comes to soften him. He
feels in every fibre of his being his own infinite
impotence, so that he can do nought but cry out,
'Lord, save me or I perish!' And while he cries,
hope comes with fluttering wings and alights
within his soul. It is the coming of the 'comforter' and 'sweet guest of the soul.' He comes
ever thus when the soul, stripped of all human
comfort, is alone in the wilderness with its
wretchedness, and can get no answer to its plaint.
Under His gentle influence hope returns, and a
man dares to trust that God can waken even his
dry bones to vigorous life. 'Come, Spirit, from
the four winds and blow upon these slain and let
them live again.' [1] And it is when a man has
thoroughly sounded the depths of his own impotence and from those depths cries out, 'Lord,
make haste to help me,' that he is really ready for
the great and divine quickening, ready—in our
Lord's words—to be 'born again' and to be born
'of God.'

In the sacraments of Baptism and Penance this
re-birth is consummated. An entirely new thing,

[1] *Ezech.* xxxvii, 9.

which is in no way part of the chain of natural causation, enters into the soul: sanctifying grace. It is purely gratuitous, an utterly unmerited thing, and one which overshoots any merely finite goal, for it is a spring of divine life and divine love. It is the work of the Holy Spirit in person, who is Himself the fulness of divine love and the great Comforter. Only in that culminating miracle of God's love, the Incarnation of the Word, is His action more fruitful, more stirring and more penetrating. The immeasurable love of God draws the soul into the circle of the divine life, so that it is vitalized as by new, divine powers, casting aside its old, earthly form of being and putting a new, super-earthly one in its place. The soul is spiritualized and interiorized after a special manner which raises it above the level of created being, and which is not to be found in the nature of even the highest seraph, but only in God Himself. That is why St. Peter speaks explicitly of our partaking of the divine nature.[1] We may call it an incarnation of God, not a literal one, nor indissoluble, but yet a true and real manifestation of God in man. God reveals Himself here, not as in creation by extraordinary signs, but in immediate self-giv-

[1] *II. Pet.* i, 4.

ing. So intimate is this manifestation of God that the soul no longer lives with its own spirit, but with the Spirit of the Son, crying 'Abba, Father.' [1] and the whole Trinity takes up its habitation in it as in a temple.

The Christian in grace is a temple of the Holy Ghost, a heaven on earth, a being of mystery, a mystery full of deep silence and devout stillness, and yet a mystery which strikes a hidden spring of vigorous life and casts a radiant beauty over the soul. The result is a new man; 'the old things are passed away; behold all things are made new.' [2] The whole personality is reorganized. Its centre of gravity is now no longer the old, earthbound self, but the new self which is bound to God in the Holy Spirit. There descends upon the soul—as at Pentecost upon the apostles—a new power, a new love, a new and stronger will. Nor does it come from ourselves. It is not already present in our desolation, or in our prayer, or in our sorrow and penance. It comes from above—like the mighty wind of Pentecost—and breaks down what is old and decayed, so that the excellency of the power of God is made manifest in earthen vessels. [3] Then is fulfilled the word of the prophet: 'I will

[1] *Gal.* iv, 6.   [2] *II. Cor.* v, 17.   [3] *II. Cor.* iv, 7.

170

give you a new heart and put a new spirit within you. I will take away the stony heart out of your body and give you a heart of flesh.' [1]

In this new heart consists Christianity's 'showing of the spirit and of power.' By means of it Christianity proves itself continuously to be the religion of the new life, the power of God entering into and transforming our world of space and time. All miracles, visions and prophecies, all exceptional manifestations that the Spirit of Pentecost still produces among the faithful, all sacraments and sacramentals, receive from this new heart their ultimate and supreme attestation. For higher than all miracles, and higher even than the sacraments is that miracle of the Holy Spirit, the re-born man, the child of God. Where this new man is not to be found, there miracles and sacraments lose their power to convince. A community which could show miracles and sacraments in abundance, but little or no trace of the new, Christian man, would be like a field of wheat with barren ears. It would not be a community of the Holy Spirit.

How does this new man reveal himself? His glad tidings is this: 'The charity of God is poured forth in our hearts by the Holy Ghost who is

[1] *Ezech.* xxxvi, 26.

given to us.'[1] His new canticle is: 'Who shall
separate us from the love of Christ? shall tribula-
tion? or distress? or famine? or nakedness? or
danger? or persecution? or the sword?'[2] How
many thousands and thousands down the centuries
have sung that song? They have looked with new
eyes upon sun and stars, upon field and flower,
upon man and beast, upon joy and sorrow. They
have loved all that is with new hearts and a new
love. Whatever is, whatever betide: God is love.
For love is the secret of all existence, of God and
of the world, of Christ and of the Church, of all
living and of all dying: the love of the Holy
Spirit, the self-subsistent, creative, eternal love, the
love which is God. Thus we come to the meaning
of those words of St. John: 'In this is love: not
as though we had loved God, but because he hath
first loved us, and sent his Son to be a propitiation
for our sins.'[3]

And with this pentecostal fire of a pure love of
God there goes also a new love of men. 'My
dearest, if God hath so loved us, we also ought to
love one another.'[4] 'There is neither Jew nor
Greek; there is neither bond nor free; there is

[1] *Rom.* v, 5. [3] *I. Jn.* iv, 10.
[2] *Rom.* viii, 35. [4] *I. Jn.* iv, 11.

neither male nor female. For you are all one in
Christ Jesus.' [1] All national, cultural, social barriers break down before this love. And it sets
free a generous and a helpful love. How doth
the love of God abide in him who hath the substance of this world and shall see his brother in
need and shall shut up his compassion from him?' [2]
The Church, the diocese, the parish: these are of
their nature fellowships in the Spirit, loving alli-
ances of men who love. And where that love is
not alive, there the fire of Pentecost is extinguished. The 'forms of piety' may remain, to use
St. Augustine's phrase, in Church, and priest and
sacrament; but their fruitful power is gone from
them. No sin or vice is so essentially inimical to
the Church, or works so destructively on her
fertility and growth as lack of charity. Are there
not signs here and there of this lack of charity?
Are there not regions within the Church that lie
barren and waste, because the Holy Spirit of in-
wardness and love has become in them an unknown
God? It was said of old: 'See how these Christians love one another,' and Christianity might well
be proud of the saying. But does it not sometimes
sound, in this our day, like a bitter reproach?

[1] *Gal.* iii, 28.   [2] *I. Jn.* iii, 17.

And yet there is nothing else to mark us out as the disciples of Jesus, but love alone. It is for the Church the supreme and, properly speaking, the sole and decisive 'showing of the spirit and of power.' No pastoral methods, or profound theology, or Christian learning can replace it. 'If I speak with the tongues of men and of angels, and have not charity, I am become as sounding brass or a tinkling cymbal.' No visions or ecstasies can replace it. 'If I should have prophecy and should know all mysteries and all knowledge, and have not charity, I am nothing.' Nor can strong faith take its place, though it manifest itself in congresses and all manner of confraternities. Were it even such a faith as could move mountains, yet would it be nothing without love. To a superficial judgment the works of ministering charity might seem to be this love, and yet not even such service is of itself sufficient. 'And if I should distribute all my goods to feed the poor, and if I should deliver my body to be burned, and have not charity, it profiteth me nothing.' [1] All associations for public service, all societies and organizations, however magnificent and comprehensive, lose all their power when they lack this one thing necessary,

[1] *I. Cor.* xiii, 1, *sqq.*

when pastor and flock have lost this pentecostal fire of a pure and mighty love of man.

'Charity is patient, is kind; charity envieth not, dealeth not perversely, is not puffed up. Is not ambitious, seeketh not her own, is not provoked to anger, thinketh no evil. Rejoiceth not in iniquity, but rejoiceth with the truth. Beareth all things, believeth all things, hopeth all things, endureth all things.' [1] 'The fruit of the spirit is love, joy, peace, patience, benignity, goodness, longanimity, mildness, modesty.' [2]

Oh, how glorious the vineyard of the Lord would be, how great its appeal, how irresistible its attraction, if all the branches of the vine bore this noble fruit of the Spirit! Then all that sought our Church would need, not to search laboriously in books and documents, but merely to ask where were the new men, the men of the new Christian love.

Come, Holy Ghost, fill the hearts of thy faithful and kindle in them the fire of thy love!

[1] *I. Cor.* xiii, 4, *sqq.*   [2] *Gal.* v, 22.

CHAPTER VII

THE WAY TO CHRIST

IT is Christmas Eve and the bells are ringing to Midnight Mass. The night is dark, but the church is ablaze with lights, and full of quietly happy folk. The mystery of Bethlehem is renewed upon the altar, and the cry goes forth: 'Christ is born to us. Come, let us adore!'

And, amid this pageantry, what am I? I am a solitary being among other such solitaries, cut off by an unbridgeable chasm from every other personality. Hence I obtain my tremendous certainty that I am, or rather, that I am not another. I am I. I am a world of my own. A mere bundle of forces? No. The lord of those forces? No, but one who ought to be the lord of those forces, and so one who is not their lord. I am one who has a war within him, I am a self at war with itself, a self that knows no peace. Above me the stars move in their regular courses, and they know whither they are going. Or rather, they do not know, but are simply moved on their way.

Whither? I do not know; nobody knows. What is the meaning of that starry world above? I do not know. It is some sort of phantasm. And nature around me, lying asleep under thick snow —is that there for me? No, the flowers will wake again in the spring, even when I am no longer there, even when there is no more any man there. Even nature that surrounds me is a phantasm. I am alone. All that I can call my own is my restlessness and inner conflict, my desire to know and my ignorance, my consciousness of duty and my impotence. In my being a thousand lines cross. They all lead beyond me, far away into space, reaching out like the naked boughs of that tree there, by the church. Whither am I going? Whence have I come? All that I know is that yesterday I was not, and to-morrow I shall have ceased to be. What am I but a failing flame, a falling wave, a dying note?

Then comes the cry from the altar: 'A Child is born to us and a Son is given to us. . . .' The Child in the manger is not like any other child, for He is God the everlasting, the all-wise, all-good, almighty; He is God the ineffable, mysterious, awful, wonderful. And has God become a child? Is the Infinite wrapped in swaddling-clothes? Is

177

the ineffable a Jewish boy, Jesus of Nazareth? Never has mouth uttered so bold an assertion. No, it is not merely bold; it is extravagance, it is blasphemy.

And yet, if it be true? If there be a God, can I argue with Him and prescribe to Him what He may or may not do? Are not my thoughts as dust before the thoughts of God? Is not all my experience a vain thing when God appears? Therefore I cannot say that it is nonsense or blasphemy to assert that God has become man. I cannot say it, because He who becomes man is God. In His thought and will are infinite possibilities, including the possibility of Bethlehem. And why should not God reveal Himself as a Child, if He reveals Himself at all? That He reveals Himself at all is the marvel, not that He reveals Himself in the form of a child. Supposing God has determined to take our human nature—and who can forbid Him? —how else should He do it but by being born as we are born, yet from a Virgin's womb? And supposing God has determined to become incarnate and thereby redeem the whole of mankind, both high and low—and who will forbid this comprehensive purpose?—could He have won the hearts of the children of men any better than by the low-

178

liness and poverty of Bethlehem? Are not poverty and lowliness the natural vesture for the divinity on earth? The purple and silk of an imperial cradle would have obscured the majesty of His divinity. How wonderful then this Christian mystery of God's condescension to the Virgin's womb! How admirable His birth in a manger! These mysteries of the Christian faith harmonize exactly with what we should expect in God's profoundest revelation of Himself.

Therefore I am not puzzled by the Child of Bethlehem, by the manger, by the swaddling-clothes. It must have been so, granted God's will to come to us. But did He will to come to us? Did the Infinite, who controls the vast universe, will to come to the tiny and insignificant planet that is called Earth? Did the All-Holy and Perfect will to come to our sin? Did the Eternal will to enter time, when Augustus was Emperor of Rome and Cyrinus governor of Syria? All understanding fails us and there is an end to our reasoning. Here is the great mystery, the miracle. And here is belief and unbelief. 'God so loved the world as to give his only-begotten Son': such is the gospel of Christmas. That is what we have to believe of God, that He loves us up to the surrender of His only-begotten Son. Surely a bold, audacious, extravagant faith! He who holds this faith believes firmly these several articles: first, that there is a living, personal God; secondly, that this God has a Son; thirdly—highest and most daring of all—that this God, blessed in His Son, stoops to our mortal clay, nay even loves it, and that so greatly, that revealing the depths of His infinite love He arrays His own Son in that same clay, so that thus clad He may redeem us.

Is such a faith, which mingles God with our mortality and makes our clay divine, a true faith, or is it not rather a travesty of faith and an insult to God? Is it not a monument of selfishness and pride? We answer that this talk of the Incarnation of the Son of God would indeed be the veriest pride and presumption, were it mere human talk. Were that so, it would be hard to find words severe enough to censure it, or to reject it with adequate indignation. But what if it is God's saying? Supposing God does really love us to such an extent that He gives us Himself in His Son. Am I so to insist on my unworthiness, and so to exaggerate my duty of reverence, that in spite of all I put away the manger, saying: 'Depart from me, O Lord, for I am a sinful man.' And what is this,

under the rags of my poverty, but a nauseous pride?
And what is my reverence but a puerile perversity?
When God holds out His gift to me, and that His
greatest gift, and that His only Son, what else
should my soul do but look up to Him from the
abyss of its unworthiness, and, ravished by His
love, answer in all humbleness and trust: 'Behold,
the handmaid of the Lord; be it done unto me
according to thy word.' Or else I am a contemner
of His gifts, and one who would presume to dic-
tate to God what He should do and what He should
leave undone. Oh; how narrow and warped are
our human judgments! Shall we never cease to
make ourselves the measure of all things, even of
the divine? But our unbelief goes deeper still, for
it attacks the very nature of the living God in His
essential attribute of generous, self-giving love.
For that is what we deny when we deny Bethlehem.
For the love of God is nowhere manifested with
such radiant purity and such overwhelming force as
in the mystery of Christmas, when all the fulness
of the Godhead dwells corporally in human form.[1]

So if we deny Bethlehem, we deny the living
God. For unbelief attacks not merely the swaddling-clothes and the manger, nor even merely the

[1] *Col.* ii, 9.

fact of the Incarnation itself, but really and fundamentally the very nature of the living God. That must be clearly recognized before we go further.

What do we mean by saying that unbelief attacks the living God? Is it really an attack, and not rather doubt, despair, search and questioning? In obstinate and assertive unbelief, there is certainly resistance and defiance. The professed atheist says: 'I will not believe.' That is the choice of his will, and his thought obeys. And why would he have no living God? Just because He is a living God. He does not object to the remote, uninterested God of the Deists. Still less does He fight against the Nature-God, or World Soul, or whatever you call the deity of pantheistic monism. He resents and attacks the living God alone. And why? Because the living God cannot be subjected to his will. He lives His own life, a life that because it is an infinite life is absolutely superior to all empirical forms of life and cannot fall within the limited range of our human experience. He cannot be seen by telescope, or discovered by microscope, or tabulated by the categories of the philosopher. There is no means whatever of circumscribing His being, of reckoning and describing it, and of submitting Him to the measure

182

of our thought. Moreover, He is such that He can at any moment break into the world of our experience with a new creation; and so all our human hypotheses and calculations are foredoomed to failure. And, finally, this living God does not leave man alone, for He makes His claims upon Him and setting in his soul the law of conscience condemns all self-will and all disobedience.

It comes to this, therefore, that the unbeliever rejects the living God because he wants his own way and wants to be exclusively himself. God is an obstacle to his egotism. He is not unlike a self-willed child which when it plays wants everything done in its own way. It resents the interference of its elders, dislikes their better thought and surer will. It wishes to build its sand-castles of its own little notions alone.

Is the unbeliever then a child? No, he is more foolish still. For he does not only resent superior mind and superior will; he rejects them utterly. That is not the temper of the child; it is sheer folly. For dispassionate reflection, revealing the 'other' to me, displays the whole universe as an incomplete and imperfect thing. On every side I discover bounds and limits, and in every direction are lines that suddenly break off. Thought is nothing else but a becoming aware of these limits, and willing is but a realization of my impotence, and feeling but a shudder at the abyss over which I hang. I am compacted of being and not being. Whatever I do has as its essential characteristic the quality of transiency; it tends to not-being. That fact is self-evident, resulting immediately from a consideration of myself, and requiring no tedious philosophy for its demonstration. On the contrary it is a necessary presupposition of any philosophy, so that it is absurd to make self the centre, to seek in self the end and meaning of existence, and, being absolutely conditioned, to think and act as though one were the Unconditioned. Consequently it is wrong from the outset to take up such an attitude of mind as hinders all honest inquiry into the ultimate end and meaning of existence, and to persist in rejecting a Life which absolutely surpasses my own. That is a proud and false self-deification which sins against the manifest law of my being; it is arrogance and rebellion.

There is therefore nothing left but that I should fairly and squarely reckon with the possibility that my little life has its origin and end in a great self-existent Life. Such is the attitude of the believer, and it alone is intelligent and honest.

184

But have I attained the living God once I have begun to reckon with the possibility of His existence? Not yet. I am on the way to Him, I have not barred the road against myself; but I have not reached Him. But can I, shall I, must I take this road? That does not depend on myself alone. Granted that there is really a living, personal God, a self-existent God, a God who is full, entire and absolute Being, then it is plain that such a God has no need of me and my faith, and that it is His pure goodness and grace if He reveals Himself to me. We should ask, therefore, not 'Shall I and must I believe?' but 'May I believe?' The inquiry after the living God must of necessity be a prayer as well as an inquiry. 'Lord, help my unbelief.' In other words, the inquiry after the personal God is never a merely philosophical inquiry; it must also be a moral and religious act. It is therefore distinct in its character from every other, such as those pursued by the natural sciences. A purely philosophical inquiry into the living God is profane and unholy, and it is therefore off the track. If there be really a living God, then I can come to Him only by prayerful thought, or better still, by thoughtful prayer. There is no other way to Him.

With this point settled, much is already settled.

We have removed those barriers of the soul which
prevent us from turning our gaze readily to God.
For there are still those among us who in the spirit
of the Voltairean epoch would surrender the sole
lordship of their soul to cold reason and trample
on the feeling of the heart; who would stifle that
deep, personal thinking which, rising up from the
depths of our being, pulsates with the fresh blood
of life. They would recognize only that thinking
which deals with the surface relations of things,
and utterly ignores substance. If there is a living
God, then I am His creature, and my whole being
is related to Him. As a consequence I can find
God only if my whole being—not thought alone,
but will and feeling also—takes part in the quest.
Or, more precisely, I can find Him only if my
inquiry is based upon the totality of my experience,
and I pursue it with a deep consciousness of my
utterly conditioned and inadequate being, which
yet by the law of its nature presses on to the absolute Being and the absolute Good. For a man to
think about God without employing at the same
time all his other spiritual faculties is about as
sensible as deciding the genuineness of a Rembrandt
by mere thought alone. And it is for this reason—
because their thought was full, personal and

living—that the men of the mediaeval, ancient, and primitive periods found God more easily than we.

Such massive thinking gives a man a new attitude towards the whole problem. Its enigma then encourages his search, its mysteriousness gives the hint of a meaning, its incoherence suggests a pattern. For my inquiry has ceased to be a hostile one, and becomes positive. From a cavilling, critical, morbid questioning, it has become constructive, comprehensive and brave.

Such questioning receives an answer from God. He answers with the countless evidences of nature. By means of that mute testimony I grasp Him with certainty as the First Cause and Self-Existent Being, as the personal Supreme Intelligence and Supreme Will.

Do I thus attain the living God of revelation, the God of Bethlehem and Christmas? No, not yet. How then do I come to this God?

I can come to the God of revelation only by His revelation. Nature may lead me up to God, but it cannot bring the living God of lavish grace down to me. Whether God has willed that I should know Him only by mute signs and as from afar, or has gone beyond that and condescended to me in a direct, living and personal manner, I can learn only from God Himself. Therefore Christmas presupposes the gospel of Christmas. But where there is a gospel, there faith is required. I must then believe.

Faith is something quite different from perception and knowledge; or rather, it *is* a perceiving and a knowing, but of an entirely different kind. If faith were not perception and a knowledge, but only a pragmatic decision born of my personal need, a deliberate closure of the debate and surrender to the Incarnate God, in order to escape from the problems of existence, from the conflict between time and eternity, matter and spirit, reason and instinct, then it would be a desperate leap into a dark unknown, and no sure pathway to a new reality. If faith is but make-believe, a holding as occurrence what cannot occur; if it be an irrational step, a self-surrender to the precise statements of an objective formula: then the whole thing looks like a deliberate shutting of one's eyes to the facts and a conscious self-deception. Why should we accept the objective statements of these formulas any more than the equally objective statements of ancient magic? But if it is not the mere objectivity of the Christmas message that inspires my faith, but its proclamation of a marvellous redemption of our afflicted nature through God's Incarnation, then my faith is not irrational. In fact it means that I have realized these three things: first that my nature is in need of redemption; secondly, that it is bound up with the ultimate mystery, that is with God; thirdly, that it is saved by the Incarnation of God. My faith is therefore illumined by reason and is a reflective faith. But is this reflective faith enough? No, it is not; because I cannot force myself to affirm the truth of the Incarnation simply because my nature requires it. A thing is not true just because I need it, for need does not create truth, but only directs us to it. Or am I forbidden to ask whether the miracle of the Incarnation is true? Must I even believe it just because it is not true for my critical thought? And is faith therefore essentially a conflict and contradiction? That could only be if God were not merely something different from me, but something essentially opposite; if my *whole* being were sin. Then I should in truth possess in myself no means of access to God. I should be darkness unpenetrated by God's light; I should be a corpse, and His life flowing round me. But am I a corpse? Am I only sin? No, I am not. I have sin, but I am not sin. I have death in me, but I am not dead. I have contrariety in me, but not pure negation, not absolute contradiction. Just for that reason my thought, for all its stumbling, can discern the problem of my being; and my will, however much it may waver, can desire the removal of my contrarieties in the God-Man. So faith in the Incarnation is not a miraculous flower growing in me without root; it has its root in my natural capacity for God, in what the theologians call a *potentia obedientialis,* and it is evoked therein by God. Therefore faith does not come to me without my co-operation. I must hold my soul ready for the living God, and I must hearken to Him when He gives testimony of Himself.

He gives that testimony through revelation. Nor should I be surprised at that, for if He is a living and personal God I should expect Him so to reveal Himself. He proves Himself to be the omnipotent and the personal God just by the fact that He reveals Himself to me in an immediate and personal way and one which goes beyond His purely objective revelation in nature. Therefore an honest and strong faith in the living God has always and everywhere become also a faith in revelation. But where there is such a revelation, there is miracle, so that the question of revelation

190

becomes the question of the miraculous. Revelation is the inroad of a new and higher truth, and it necessarily flashes out in miracle. So the question of the miraculous is intimately connected with the truth of the revelation, and—further still—with the real existence of a living, personal God. Because of this intimate connection with faith, the question of the miraculous has a special religious quality.

In this attitude of mind I turn my attention to Christianity. First of all I seek to regard it comprehensively and grasp it as a complete manifestation, without testing every detail. As such a complete manifestation I compare it with the other religions through which men have sought in the course of the centuries to satisfy their craving for holiness and God. At once I observe the surpassing quality of its fundamental attitude, and the sublimity of its dogma, morality and worship; and the more I compare it with other religions the more plain does its superiority become. The Christian faith is a lofty one, unsullied by any coarse or fantastic quality, and yet it does not despise the body or indulge in inhuman condemnation of our natural life. In it the most daring aspirations are realized, the most intimate yearnings of the soul, the bravest ideals, the purest devotion. If mankind were but able and willing to live according to the spirit of Christianity, it would be completely happy. So, having gained this appreciation of the sublimity of Christianity, I am disposed to examine its historical origins. These origins are inseparably bound up with the appearance of a figure, which—however imperfect tradition about Him may be—displays the ideal of a pure, holy, wise, good, courageous, perfect humanity in so luminous and impressive, yet so simple and plain a fashion, that He is for always the ideal man. Of this ideal figure His most intimate friends and disciples tell us that He described Himself as the Son of the Father, and that He went to death with the definite purpose of giving Himself as a 'redemption for many.' And attributing these claims to their Master, they attribute to Him also a life and activity of an unusual and very individual sort. They tell of miracles wrought on sinners, on the sick, and on the dead. These miracles, as they describe them, are devoid of any of that ostentation and quackery which mark the performances of contemporary wonder-workers. They have the character rather of radiant love, and of holiness showing itself amid misery and poverty. Nor are they mere casual occurrences in the life of Jesus;

192

on the contrary they are true reflections of His
inward nature and are most intimately connected
with His person. This miraculous quality of His
person and work reaches a climax in His Resurrection. That miracle, while it marks the end of
His human life, reveals at the same time its inward
consistency and meaning, and can be understood in
its convincing power only in connection with that
life. The whole Person of Jesus, that manifestation of holiness, of newness, of power and purity,
which is so securely attested by history, gives to
the narratives of the Resurrection—which so many
thousands have affirmed with their deaths—their
place in the story and the power they have of re-
acting on the life itself, illuminating it and making
it credible. In the light of His life, the Resurrection of Jesus is seen to be a solemn divine con-
firmation of this life, the solution of the riddle of
His person, the decisive word on His mystery.

But the inquirer may not be entirely satisfied
even with the testimony of our Lord's Resurrection. The Resurrection as a historical event belongs to the past; but, if I am to achieve a true
personal relation to Jesus, the Resurrection must
be made present to me, and not only the Resurrection, but His whole life. Otherwise the best I

can achieve is a respectful admiration and awe for a very remarkable, miraculous figure. Moreover, if He was really God, then He must have exercised creative power, He must have originated something, given birth to a new movement and sent forth a stream of new life. So I want a present reality, a present divine life.

Can this divine life of the Risen Christ be found upon the earth? All true life is creative life, for life enkindles life. Of its nature it tends to propagate itself, to take new forms, to develop; but always preserving its organic unity. For life, though ever growing, yet remains ever true to itself. Is there upon the earth any such life as this that we can trace to the divine power of the Risen Christ? If He be truly risen, there must be such a life. And the life originated by Him must be the life of an infinitely fruitful organic unity, of a vital fellowship. It cannot be found in individuals and solitary units, but only in the flowing life of a great, holy fellowship.

So I seek for such a fellowship, in which Christ's life and Resurrection are a living force, in which the Jesus of history achieves His totality and fulness.

Many societies call themselves after His name, but where is His totality, where His creative fulness? My principle of selection can only be that of creative fellowship, of unity in fulness. When life is full and rich, and yet for all its fulness is consciously one, eminently individual, completely self-consistent: then I know for certain that I am in the presence of genuine, creative life.

If I look into the past, if I consider the present, if I speculate on the future, there is one obvious answer to my question—the world-embracing Catholic Church. Wherever I turn I meet her imposing presence. That Church alone, through the series of its popes and bishops, reaches back in direct line, a line that has never been broken or violently deflected, to Jesus and His disciples. Through it alone can I obtain a true historical sympathy with Jesus. Without it the gospel of the miracle-worker who rose again from the dead would be a strange and beautiful tale from a bygone age. But it brings Jesus into the immediate present; He is made present to the living faith, the unconquerable, undying hope, and the burning love of all the Christian generations, who united across the abyss of time into one single great fellowship, cry with one heart and one tongue to Jesus: 'Thou hast the words of eternal life.'

Nor does the Catholic Church merely confess its

faith in Jesus; it possesses Him in its sacred mysteries. It knows that it is really and truly conjoined with Him, flesh of His flesh, spirit of His spirit; that it is His fulness and His body. Not even his own mother, nor his own child, is so nigh to the Catholic, so familiar, so profoundly intimate as Jesus is. He was and is the King of all hearts. Here indeed is creative life, the continuously manifest life of the Risen Christ. If I enter this stream of life then I touch Christ Himself, like the woman with the issue of blood who touched the hem of His garment, or like St. Thomas when he put his finger into the wound of His side. The Jesus of yesterday becomes to me the Jesus of to-day, the Redeemer, whom I can as it were see with my own eyes and hear with my own ears, even as the apostles did. Every word of His is now a word spoken to me by Himself, and becomes to me 'spirit and life.' Thus the Catholic Church in its continuous life puts Jesus above the changes of time and maintains the living spirit of His word. It is the on-moving life of the Risen Christ; it is Christ unfolding Himself in history; it is the fulness of Christ.

And in its fulness it is also one. By its unity it shows that it is not merely a broad stream of life, but that it has depth, and steadfast self-control, so that it abides always true to itself and can never lose its essential nature. By its persistent unity it shows that it is the vigorous life that springs from the one Holy Spirit of God. In duality and plurality there is division and dissension, and the true Spirit of Jesus is not at work, but a human, separatist spirit. All are not one in Christ, and each individual eats his own bread, not the bread that makes all into one body. Every dissension, every breaking off from the original unity, inevitably bears upon it the mark of the non-divine, of the purely human and selfish. The Catholic Church is not dissension, nor a plurality of opinions, nor individualism, but a fellowship in time and space, a fellowship that is not the mere sum total of its units, or a harmonious concord of discordant views, but an essential fellowship, which as a supra-personal unity is prior to its individual members and forms the basis of their union. This supra-personal unity is rooted in the one Spirit of Jesus, in the fulness of His creative truth and grace. This life-giving fulness flows with an exuberant fecundity through all peoples and civilizations, purifying, stimulating, shaping, pervading; but, because it comes from the Heart of

197

Jesus, it never loses itself and its supernatural character. We should liken it, therefore, not to a grain of gold discovered in some mass of alien rock, but to a living seed which takes up foreign elements into itself and employs them for the building up of its own structure, yet always and ever according to the law of its being. And to this supernatural character of the Church's being there corresponds the supernatural quality of the means through which that being works. The dogma, sacraments, and authority of the Church are supra-personal things, and only so does the truth and grace of Christ remain unaffected by the human agent. The centuries pass and new generations are constantly arising; throughout all changes it is never Peter, or Paul, or Pius that preaches and baptizes, but always and everywhere Christ. This supernatural principle of unity pervades the whole visible Church and every part of it. The one Christ prayed for the one visible Peter that his faith might not fail, and upon the one visible Peter rests the whole visible Church. He supports and guards its unity. Through him its unity is realized and made manifest. He is the steward of that one bread which makes the many into one body.

So my Christmas faith implies the sacred triad: God, Christ, the Church. God reveals Himself to my mind and conscience in the works of nature; but that He also communicates Himself to me beyond the course of nature I learn from Jesus Christ, in whom God appeared in human form. To Christ Himself, and to a faithful grasp and hold of the divinity that was manifested in Him, I come, not merely mediately through literary records, but decisively and immediately in the Church, which is informed by His life and shows itself in its continuous, unbroken, vital unity as the genuine production of His vivifying spirit, as His fulness. 'I have God for my Father,' said St. Cyprian, 'because I have the Church for my mother.'

The consequence follows naturally that a man who stands outside this living Catholic fellowship is a solitary and isolated person. He may unite with like-minded people and form a fellowship apart from the Church. But such associations, depending upon individual will and designed to meet individual needs, are purely human structures and are not established by the Spirit of Christ. For this Spirit, by the law of its nature, must reveal itself in all the stages of its historical unfolding as creative fellowship, unity and love, as always the

199

'Body of Christ.' There can be no other manifestation of the Spirit of Christ, and therefore all
schismatics and heretics isolate themselves from
that Spirit. Their fellowships are of their own
making and are not the creation of God; and so,
like a piece of living tissue that is severed from an
organism, they may live on for a while by some
artificial process, but they cannot live for long, or
display creative vitality.

Certainly the Spirit of God breathes where He
will. That Spirit visits the individual and the
solitary, the Jew and the Gentile, but never otherwise than as a Spirit of love and fellowship, as a
Spirit that is constantly working towards the full
and complete unity of the brethren. Christ's Spirit
can never abide in a society that sets itself up
against the unity and love of His Church, so that
even the professedly 'social' Christian may be a
solitary. As a bright light set in a room throws
its rays through the windows and illumines the
dark street outside, so is it with the Catholic
Church. The dark path of many a non-Catholic
Christian is lit up by scattered rays that fall upon
it from Christ's fellowship and the Church of His
grace. Such a one lives by the Church, though he
may be hostile to it. And were that fellowship to

be destroyed, then the little light that is in him would go out, even as the satellite star is involved in the extinction of its sun.

But far more isolated still is the man who insists on living his life entirely alone and seeking his own way. He shuts out deliberately any influence of the living fellowship of Christ, and supposes that the only road to truth is the road of literary records. He is like a man who deliberately closes his eyes to the splendours of spring, and prefers to infer its glory from the dead leaves of autumn. Such a man, assuredly, has before him a long, hard and hopeless quest, a desperate wrestling with God. And it may happen that this wrestling becomes at last an end in itself, a sort of mimic war against God. The man sets himself to test whether God can break down his defences and compel him to believe. Or he treats God as nothing better than a sum or a riddle, the solution of which has been set men for their life task. And he behaves as though man had to decide the fate of God. It is playing the part of those giants who fought against heaven, a silly and unworthy and childish game, however much braggadocio we may put into it. For we are not Prometheus, and if we were, God does not let his fire be stolen from Him. And so it happens that no one makes so much ado about God as do these solitary fighters with God; and yet no one finds God so seldom.

The Catholic on the other hand is never solitary. He never flees into solitude to seek God and test Him. He lives always in the fulness and fellowship of the Church, wherein Christ is vitally perpetuated.

And therefore, so long as he does not allow himself to be divorced from his fellowship by the mad rush of life and the still madder craze for 'autonomous' thinking, he is preserved from such errors as we have been considering. He will not lightly ignore that constant manifestation of God which appears in the living faith of the Church, or make the bold demand that God, if He wants to be recognized, should reveal Himself anew to pure thought. His mentality is far different from that of the modern egoist. Having a deep consciousness of his own insufficiency, a respect for the data of nature and history, a lively appreciation of holiness and ideal virtue, some experience of the power of a truly Christian life to purify, elevate and make happy, but above all a living sympathy with the faith of the Communion of Saints of all times and places—he is safe against the attacks of serious doubt. A Catholic is a man of positive temper; he tends to affirm rather than to deny. And he makes his affirmation in a comprehensive fashion, with every power of his own being and in union with all his brethren in that mighty fellowship. And so his faith, because it has this character, is neither an unattainable nor an uncertain thing; on the contrary it is solid conviction, sure affirmation, peace in the truth.

But we must not suppose that this peace in the truth, which is characteristic of Catholicism, is merely a dull, easy-tempered, mentally indolent acceptance of the revelation which the Church sets before us. For the Catholic enlists not reason only, but his whole personality, in the business of believing, and into his act of faith he puts the best of his being. His faith is an acceptance of the living God who reveals Himself in the Church through His Son, an acceptance which is characterized by sincerity, reverence, humility, love and courage. A mere acceptance of doctrine as true just for tradition or habit's sake is not genuine Catholic faith, and is not distinguishable from the similar acceptance and transmission of purely secular traditions and customs. Faith is an act and must be reiterated again and again. Indeed it may sometimes become a hard conflict, as for instance when a Catholic lives in an atmosphere of criticism and contradiction and finds his faith subjected to those solvent forces. His faith then becomes a wrestling for God which taxes all his powers; but it can never become a wrestling against God, in which God is first violently excluded from the soul in order that this exclusion having been effected he may face the problem without any presuppositions. His Mother, the Church, has his hand in hers, he is immersed in the abundant life of the Communion of Saints, he cannot examine his faith otherwise than from out of that rich life, than in this fellowship and through it. He will inquire and investigate with the experience of love; he will seek contact with the living Church, and he will keep in contact with it. And the grace of faith which is granted to the children of the Church will give his soul such light and strength that it will be saved from all erroneous answers and solutions.

Does Catholic faith, then, depend in the last resort upon the Church alone? If the question implies that the Church is the ultimate basis of the certitude of faith, then it has already been answered in what has been said, and we have not alleged that the Catholic could or might regard the visible Church as the ultimate, decisive basis of his faith. As a visible fellowship the Church guards, attests, explains, defends my faith in the living God revealed in Christ; but the Church is not the deepest ground of that faith. The Church itself is inspired by the Spirit of Christ, the Spirit of God, and it is really that Spirit that I believe and trust. I grasp in one comprehensive view all the forces that work upon my mind, will, heart and whole being, raising, deepening and fulfilling, and that pulsate through the visible Church in its ministration of doctrine and sacrament; and I can interpret these forces only as the evidence of a truly divine life. It is therefore ultimately not the visible Church that I believe, but God working through Christ in His Church. I believe God for His own sake.

But how do I know that it is God that I believe? Not having met God face to face, how can I say that it is God? We have already seen in outline how we can reach a general belief in God; and this further conviction that God works in the Church may be reached in much the same way. An impartial consideration of the data of nature and history enables me to conclude from the form taken by Christianity and the Church—a form which defies naturalistic explanation—that they must be God's work, or else the universe is irrational. I cannot believe that behind so much sincerity and earnestness, so much insight and spirituality, so many signs and testimonies, so much courage, purity, fecundity and power, there stands a delusion and a gross deception. The deception of the apostles and other witnesses of the faith would recoil upon God Himself. Under the surface of things there would be nothing but sheer nonsense. And my own nature, with its longing to discover the ultimate meaning of things, would be a tormenting riddle. I cannot believe that that is so. It would be a mad leap into chaos, or rather into absolute nothingness. It would be self-annihilation, the deification of unreason and universal madness. So my intuitive certitude that in the Church I meet God depends to that extent in the last resort upon a postulate: my intellectual and moral nature require me to believe so.

But my faith is far more than such a postulate as this, so deeply tinged with pessimism and scepticism. It is a seeing and a tasting, a true seeing though it be 'through a mirror.' [1] I do not, of course, grasp the supernatural object of faith in its

[1] *I. Cor.* xiii, 12.

own essence. But I track it in its effects, in the unparelleled purity, depth and power with which 'the spirit himself giveth testimony to our spirit, that we are the sons of God.' [1] I perceive it also outside myself in that "odour of life unto life' [2] which emanates from the Church's mysteries, from its austere doctrine, from its stern discipline and from its unnumbered saints. I can to some degree test my faith by experience. And the more expressly I live by the Gospel, the more does my experimental certitude grow that it is the 'power of God unto salvation to everyone that believeth.' [3]

I grant that such certitude as this will never be an exact certitude in the strict sense of the word. Purely human insight can never be so rich and deep as formally to compel us to believe in God and in His word. [4] Our religious thinking will ever remain burdened by obscurities. How then do we come nevertheless to a full and firm belief? We do so not through the power of our thinking, but through the might of our willing. For faith is not mere knowledge; it is also an act of decision, an act of the will. Since our will of its very nature is occupied with the realm of values, it is necessary

---

[1] *Rom.* viii, 16.   [2] *II. Cor.* ii, 16.   [3] *Rom.* i, 16.
[4] **Vatican Council, Session III.,** *De fide,* **Canon 5.**

only that the Supreme Good should but lightly touch the responsive soul, and the human will turns itself to Him in free act, and with the power of its decision carries the hesitating mind over the dark places and compels it to assent. So I believe because I will to believe. From out of the depth of my vital will I affirm that God whom my thought descries as from afar.

But why do I decide for God and His truth, and why do so many other people refuse to believe, though they have God's revelation as much as I? This question leads us to the last and deepest point of all, a point indeed that is buried in the mystery of divine predestination. For our Lord Himself said: 'No man can come to me, unless it be given him by my Father.' [1] My faith, however much it be my own act, is yet on the other hand in a very true sense wrought by God. 'For by grace you are saved through faith. And that not of yourselves, for it is the gift of God.' [2] My faith is in its ultimate foundations the grace and gift of God.

Does that mean that it is not a man's fault if he refuses faith? When we ask that question we come up against the mystery of divine election, and for

[1] *Jn.* vi, 66.   [2] *Eph.* ii, 8.

that mystery there is no solution on this earth. This much only may we say, that unbelief would be no fault if God's influence in this choice were on all fours with our willing and were exerted in the same plane of being. In that case, since God is the initial agent, and from eternity calls one man to belief effectively, and another ineffectively, He would have to bear the sole responsibility for man's unbelief. But God's influence is not so exerted. For while His being and His will embrace and dominate mine, yet they do so in such a way that my being is not destroyed nor my will enslaved. Such is the unsearchable sublimity of God's creative power that He has made a reasonable being which is wholly His and yet belongs wholly to itself. And in the supernatural order He effects a faith which is wholly His gift, and yet on the other hand is wholly man's affair. Our belief or unbelief is wholly and entirely our own doing, and yet at the same time wholly and entirely God's. And only because our belief or unbelief is wholly God's doing is it truly and really our belief or unbelief. For grace does not exclude responsibility nor does responsibility exclude grace. We are assuredly responsible for our unbelief, for our Lord has said: 'He that believeth not the Son shall not see life, but the wrath of God abideth on him.' [1] And yet that other saying of His is no less true: 'No man can come to me, except the Father, who hath sent me, draw him.' [2] The mystery of faith goes down into the mystery of God.

[1] *Jn.* iii, 36.   [2] *Jn.* vi, 44.